RACE AGAINST TIME

CLAIRE ECKARD
WITH KYLA & NATALIE LAW

PLAIN SIGHT PUBLISHING
An imprint of Cedar Fort, Inc.
Springville, Utah

What others are saying about this book . . .

Nothing can seem to bond two people more than a love of horses and an open trail. Emotionally I rode with Kyla and Flash over Cougar Rock, in and out of the hot canyons. I held my breath at the veterinarian check points as she did. And then, with the Tevis Cup moon as the guiding light, Kyla and Flash's journey ends. A hundred miles completed, and you know in your heart that had the trail been longer, the two of them would have been up to the challenge. You sigh with envy.

—JULIE SUHR, author of *Ten Feet Tall, Still*
Twenty-five-time Tevis Cup finisher,
"Grande Dame" of endurance

Race against Time is a riveting story of faith, tenacity, and adventure as a young girl and a wild Hackney pony overcome adversity and find real adventure in this "against all odds" true story. From the gripping start to the exciting finish, readers are quickly drawn into Kyla and Flash's world where in their struggle, each finds in the other a bond of strength, friendship, and purpose. The readers are inspired to appreciate the individual challenges they each face, and how their faith in one another galvanized their never-give-up attitude as they make history in one of the world's toughest endurance races. This book is for horse lovers, but it's also for all of those who embody a spirit of adventure and an appreciation for the bond that two souls can forge by overcoming challenges together, learning to trust one another on this unique and challenging journey. The strong relationship between Kyla, her mother, and her extended family and group of friends is engaging and highlights the importance of community. The photographs are illustrative of the intensity of this event and offer a great visual support of Eckard's beautifully written text.

—DR. LUCIAN SPATARO JR., PhD,
author of "The Long Ride" and director
of the Center for Political Thought and
Leadership, Arizona State University

A remarkable story artfully told of highly effective parenting. You'll love Kyla, adore her pony, and cheer for her mom.

—KIRK MAGLEBY, executive director,
Book of Mormon Central

Claire has captured the essence of endurance riding. It is not a sport. It is a lifestyle. Page after page, I felt that she was plucking words and thoughts right out of my head. A fun read and a memory ignitor. Job well done! Thank you!

BART ESKANDER, Emmy Award-winning
director of *The Price is Right*, two-time Tevis finisher

This skillfully written book about the unpretentious pair of Kyla Law and her Hackney pony, Flash, is captivating. Set against the backdrop of endurance riding and the most arduous trail across the Sierra Nevada Mountains, they dazzled everyone with their hard-earned finish at the Tevis Cup Ride. Apart from being wildly inspirational, this story elaborates on the degree of perseverance and determination required to accomplish such a heroic challenge. It sets a great example for anyone, and especially the next generations of endurance riders. It's an essential addition to any impassioned equestrian's library.

—SHANNON YEWELL WEIL, author of Strike A Long Trot–
Legendary Horsewoman Linda Tellington-Jones

I was on the Cup committee in 2021. I first noticed Kyla and Flash at the pre-ride veterinary check at Robie Park. I have memories of a couple of POA ponies, as well as an Icelandic (horse) or two during my over 50 years of association with the famous 100-mile ride, but when I saw the tiny Hackney pony called Flash, I couldn't imagine how such a small creature would be able to negotiate the rough, mountainous trail, especially carrying a rider up and over Cougar Rock. As the day progressed, the little guy seemed to get stronger and stronger. The long-legged, small girl also looked better than most of the adults, especially during the extreme heat of the day. The beautiful Mom, Natalie, seemed to be very much in control, as I thought of the responsibility of taking a child, especially on a small pony, over that trail! Claire has captured the true essence and spirituality of the trail. From start to finish, it is a journey of NO return, as well as the challenge of a lifetime. Kyla and her journey of overcoming the bullies and mean kids at school to her dedication and never-give-up attitude when presented with a feral pony and a big challenge is a fabulous example for individuals of all ages! The family's faith in God and wholesome family values is something rarely seen these days! Congratulations to all of you, and Claire, for capturing the true meaning of "endurance," not only on a treacherous trail, but in life in general! Never give up!!!!

—DIANE (RUNNING DEER) RIPLEY, Dubois, Wyoming,
author of Return to the River, endurance rider, and
Tevis Cup committee member

The story of Kyla and Flash should be read by every girl who ever loved a horse. As well, every mother with a daughter will want to read the story of victory over hard life lessons and the joy that perseverance brings. This is a poignant tale that I can't wait to share with my daughters, and with theirs.

—LAURIE BOAZ, AQHA and NRCHA competitor

Race against Time is the powerful and heartwarming story of a bullied, outcast young woman (Kyla) and a neglected, mistreated horse (Flash) and how this dynamic duo comes together to motivate, encourage, and ultimately heal each other as they set out to achieve something extraordinary.

—CHRIS HEIMERDINGER, author of the Tennis Shoes
Adventure Series, producer, LDS Top Ten Author

As a 25 Tevis buckle recipient, I found this to be a remarkable true-life journey of a young girl, a pony, and a mom. It holds some real-life adventures as well as some amazing life lessons about faith and the rewards of perseverance . . . A MUST READ.

—KATHIE PERRY, 25-time Tevis finisher

Claire Eckard enlightens us by providing her insight to the world's most demanding long-distance equestrian endurance contests through the dreams, hopes, and efforts of Kyla Law and her Hackney pony, Flash. Along with her mother and her horse, Kyla finds herself with the lofty goal of planning and preparing for the ultimate test of horsemanship of their first attempt in conquering the Western States Trail through the rugged Sierra Nevada from Lake Tahoe to Auburn, California. The Tevis Cup 100-Mile One-Day Ride is terribly honest in its demands and rewards. Having encountered these before, I can affirm that one achieves more in victory or defeat than in staying home to risk neither. By the time they reached the finish, Flash and Kyla, along with her mother, found as many valleys and peaks both physically and mentally as mark this trail. Kyla and Flash proved that honor lay not so much in having the courage and fitness to reach the finish line as in daring to arrive at the start!

—HAL V. HALL, three-time winner of the Lloyd Tevis Cup,
three-time recipient of the James Ben Ali Haggin Cup,
31-time Tevis Ride finisher, and American Endurance
Ride Conference Hall of Famer

I have just finished *Race against Time*. What a spiritual adventure! The description of the Tevis trail and the strength it takes to complete it shone in every chapter. Kyla Law and her mother, Natalie, shared a mother-daughter experience they will always treasure. The book spoke of the essence of the sport of endurance and what it entails, and I have never seen the Tevis trail spoken of so thoroughly or so eloquently written. As a fellow adventurer, I loved the book!

—TOM SITES, the Great American Horse Race of 1976 finisher;
four-time finisher of the Old Dominion 100 mile endurance ride;
Team Gold Medal at European Championships; True Grit
award at the North American Championships 1989 and 2,000;
the European Championships in Marloffstein Germany
in 1987; North American Championships in Ontario,
Canada, top ten; and the True Grit award in
1989, 2,000 AERC miles

A must-read for horse lovers! *Race against Time* opens an incredible window into the world of endurance riding. A bold and beautiful story. You will find yourself rooting for Kyla and Flash as they ride through each of life's challenges, including a race that most equestrians only dream about!

—ALYSSA MATHEWS, award-winning filmmaker
and founder of DiscoverTheHorse

I have always felt the sport I love and participate in is like an unknown world to many other people. Now, however, here is Claire Eckard, writing beautiful stories about endurance riding and putting this incredibly challenging and exciting sport on the world map for all to enjoy. There are so many brave and athletic legendary characters, both horse and human, in this discipline that should be written about that Claire will have her work cut out for her for many years to come. Here we have a wonderful true story of a little pony and her young rider taking on the most challenging endurance event in the world. What a story it is, and captured so brilliantly with Claire's writing. The grit, determination, fitness, and commitment and love of your horse (or pony) are captured here, proving that without such skills, no horse or human would ever finish 100 miles. Perhaps now horsey and non-horsey people alike will understand the true essence of the passionate world of endurance riding and understand that "to finish is to win."

SALLY FENNER, author, top twenty Tevis finisher

For so many of us endurance isn't simply a sport, it's a lifestyle, and something that becomes a big influence on how we look at life regardless of if we realize it or not. Claire has captured this perfectly in the story of Kyla and Flash in both their journey to Tevis and over those mountains. A true reminder that anything is possible with the right mindset.

—TAHLIA FRANKE, 2022 100-mile Quilty Cup winner, Australia

Everyone loves an underdog story, especially when they are true! As a movie producer of films based on true stories, there is nothing that I love more than to see people inspired by real events. A girl, a pony, and the toughest 100-mile race in the world. What more could you want! This is an amazing adventure, and I am extremely excited that this story is being told. I think you will love it as much as I do!

—MICHAEL DAVIS, movie producer (p.g.a.)

Beautiful, well written, and easy to follow, vet check to vet check like I've never read. Good read, I liked it.

—CURT LEWIS, journalist, author of *The Great American Horse Race of 1976*

Girl gets pony, girl rides pony, girl outgrows pony. This is a typical scenario throughout time, but the story of Kyla and Flash is anything from typical. Kyla's love and persistence was able to break through Flash's distrust of people, in doing so, made them a record-setting team. The ever-growing Kyla rode Flash to an impressive finish at the grueling Tevis Cup 100-mile endurance ride through the Sierra Nevada. At 11.2 hands, Flash is the smallest equine to ever complete the ride in its 66-year history.

A Race against Time is a beautiful story of love, faith, persistence, and overcoming challenges. It will inspire and encourage others to never give up and to reach for the stars.

—LORI OLESON, endurance rider, author of
Endurance . . . Years Gone By, Enduring Memories,
over 14,000 competitive miles

An inspirational true story of hope, horses, and making dreams come true. Claire has captured the magic of falling in love with a horse, overcoming the odds, and achieving the impossible. Everyone who has ever ridden a horse, or even longed to pat one, will enjoy sharing this journey with Kyla and the pony, Flash, as they meet, become partners, and conquer one of the greatest horse-and-rider challenges in the world—the Tevis Cup. An entertaining and well-written book containing powerful messages about the nature of horses, people, and life itself. Kyla and Flash reminded me that anything is possible when the hearts of giants reside in small bodies. I think we all need more inspirational stories like this to keep us positive in difficult times.

—LEANNE OWENS (B.A., Grad.Dip.Ed., M.Ed.), author
of *The Dimity Horse Mysteries* and *The Outback Riders,*
writer/reporter for *Horse Talk TV*, and winner
of scores of national and state titles with her horses

What a beautiful testimony of how love, trust, and faith can change hearts, give courage, and lead to wonderful memories and grand achievements. It's easy to picture the absolutely stunning scenery, feel the atmosphere during the endurance rides, and experience the emotions throughout this journey while reading the book. The adventures of this brave young girl and her "fire-breathing pocket dragon" Hackney pony will light a fire in any heart. We loved reading about your journey, Kyla, Flash, and Natalie. Here's to many more such great adventures in the future!

—GILLIAN WILLEMSE, Pandora Performance Saddles, sponsor

The book captures everything about the Tevis Cup, from the months of hard training to the ride itself. What a wonderful story—a young girl, a wild Hackney pony, and their Tevis Cup journey. Watching them check in at Robie Park and then witnessing their finish at McCann Stadium in Auburn was a real treat! Now, reading their backstory makes their story just so much more special!

—MIKE PERALEZ, DVM, head vet, Tevis Cup

Race against Time tells a captivating story about a girl and her horse while highlighting the versatility and natural athleticism of the American Saddlebred."

—DAVID MOUNT, executive director/CEO, American
Saddlebred Horse and Breeders Association

When my son was born some forty-two years ago, my elderly old granddad Cox said, "I only have this word of advice for raising kids: never hold a kid back." I like to think with my limited resources I offered him every opportunity to advance himself, explore his options, test, feel, and try to find his place in life. He skied, took piano, rode horses, rode a motorcycle, climbed trees, rode a bicycle, swam, ran, and took karate—all before age ten. He was in college determined to be an elementary school teacher. He died in a car accident at age nineteen, never seeing his career choice come to fruition.

I met Natalie Law and her children several years ago through the horse world and have followed them on FaceBook ever since. Natalie and her husband, Adam, may have heard

Granddad Cox's advice, because they sure never hold any of their kids back! They are raising hardworking, capable, reliable, self-sufficient, and driven children who are fearless, educated, and as well-rounded as any children you'd hope to meet.

Kyla Law at age thirteen is an enigma and a dedicated young horse woman. Like her siblings, she is athletic. She swims, jumps into water from VERY high places, competes in cross country foot race events, dances, sings, and raises animals, but above all, she loves to ride and train her horses!

Natalie is an advanced horsewoman having ridden in multiple endurance events, but one of her biggest achievements has been to nurture the inner drive of Kyla, who has ridden them all with her. At age twelve, Kyla announced her desire to ride the Tevis Cup, a 100-mile extremely challenging endurance race across the Sierra Nevada Mountain range on her pony, Flash! Qualifying for the Tevis Cup meant lots of condition riding, extreme focus on the care and nutrition needs of the horse, and finishing several qualifying rides leading up to the event! And Flash was a pony-sized horse.

There was never any doubt in my mind that Natalie and Kyla would succeed! At age thirteen, Kyla was one of the youngest people to ever finish this world-famous event, with Flash setting a new record as the smallest horse to ever finish.

To say I have always admired and been proud of this family is an understatement, and I often share their stories and life adventures on my social media pages. This book will show others what I know already—that Kyla, Flash, and the entire Law family are extraordinary people who once they set their mind on a goal will overcome everything standing in their way to achieve it. I am very proud to share Kyla's next great adventure. *Race against Time* shares four years of her and Flash's life, with all the raw emotion and multiple challenges they had to overcome as they prepared for the toughest endurance race in the world—the Tevis Cup.

—GERRY COX, professional top-ranked horse trainer,
grand champion reining, working cow horse,
and trail challenge, and was featured on "Best
of America by Horseback," *RFD-TV*

About Gerry Cox

Gerry Cox has been riding, training, and competing with horses much of his adult life and has won at endurance races in team roping, calf roping, and was a grand champion in reining, working cow horse, and trail challenges. Gerry has studied under sixteen world champion horsemen. These include Al Dunning and Les Vogt and four Road to the Horse champions—Chris Cox, Craig Cameron, Dan James, and Jim Anderson. Gerry has been a top contender at the Extreme Mustang Makeover. Top contender at Colt Start Challenge Events. Top contender at Craig Cameron Extreme Cowboy Races. Clinician at BLM Wild Mustang Gentling Demonstrations. Featured Clinician on continued . . . "Best of America By Horseback" (*RFD-TV*). He has served as judge at the National Finals Rodeo Colt Starting Championships. He was one of ten horsemen selected to compete in the Charles Wilhelm Super Horse Challenge. View some of Gerry's work at www.YouTube.com (Gerry Cox Horse). Find Gerry on FaceBook.

Cover photo credit: © Gore/Baylor Photography—Bill Gore

ISBN 13: 978-1-4621-4404-4

Published by Plain Sight Publishing, an imprint of Cedar Fort, Inc.
2373 W. 700 S., Suite 100, Springville, UT 84663
Distributed by Cedar Fort, Inc., www.cedarfort.com

Library of Congress Control Number: 2022946427

Cover design by Shawnda T. Craig
Cover design © 2023 Cedar Fort, Inc.
Horse graphic on page 183 courtesy of Woodcutter

Printed in the United States of America

10 9 8 7 6 5 4 3 2 1

Printed on acid-free paper

CONTENTS

ACKNOWLEDGMENTS

FROM NATALIE LAW

I've been a horse owner for nine years, and I've been riding endurance for only six of those. That is such a short time in the horse world. In those years I feel I've been relatively successful, but 100 percent of that success has come from the willingness of others to share their knowledge and experience. Over the past six years of endurance riding, I've had the opportunity to ride with, and pick the brains of, the best of the best—the legends of endurance, some would say.

First, I want to thank Shelah Wetter. She started as my tiny kids' riding instructor. I would sit in the middle of the indoor arena bundled up in as many layers as possible with the big, furry barn cat on my lap to keep me warm, while all my kids would run amuck watching Shelah teaching Kyla to ride. Later she taught all three of my girls to ride. I'd watch the way she calmly handled situations, the way she would firmly correct yet always leave the student feeling like they were on top of the world. Our relationship grew from her being my kids' instructor to my instructor, and then to my friend. Shelah was with me from the start of my adult horse career to when we crossed the Tevis finish line in Auburn in July 2021. I can't thank her enough for all she has done, and continues to do, for me and my family.

Next, I'd like to thank Dave (The Duck) and Annie Nicholson, who have a special place in my heart. Not only do they manage the most beautiful rides, but they also truly desire to see success and enjoyment in their riders. Their ride camps foster a place where the entire family is welcomed, and kids can run free and enjoy this beautiful earth. I have spent hours picking Dave's brain, either at ride camps or on the phone, and he has always been generous with his time and advice, sharing anything and everything that will help us and our horses. Their rides also attract the best of the best in the endurance world.

At these rides I've had the opportunity to ride with and learn from so many, and I'm thankful for the time they've spent sharing their knowledge with me. I have a list a mile long of people to thank. If I tell a story about each and every one of them, we'll have a separate novel, so I'm going to make a nice long list here. These people in some way or another have a place in my heart for what they've shared with me. They may already know the impact they had on Kyla and me, or reading this may be the first time they even knew we existed, but to us, they mean something.

Roshelle Bromley
Dave Rabe
Lindsay Fisher
Naomi Preston
Crockett Dumas
Cassee Terry
Lorie Stobie
Darlene and Max Merlich
Dennis and Sue Summers
Sandra and Guy Cheek
John and Diane Stevens
Kathleen Pilo
Kim Elkins
Kacey Oar

Tennessee Lane and SoCo Endurance
John Perry
Stacy Pratt and Heartland Scootboots
Hoof Armor
Carrie Moyers and Horse Bums
Pandora Performance Saddles
XP Rides
PNER (Pacific Northwest Endurance Riders)
EDRA (Equine Distance Riding Association)
AERC (American Endurance Ride Conference)

I also want to thank the most important people in my life—my family. First, my husband, Adam Law, for never holding me back from what I set my heart on, and my parents, James and Wynona Mayer, for raising me to be the woman I am today. They taught me that "try" is a powerless word, so I should just get out and "do." Because of them I never question "if" I can do something because I know that I can do anything. And last, I thank my God above, my Heavenly Father, for everything I have been blessed with in this life. Not a day goes by out on my horses that I don't give thanks to God for all His creations and for the opportunities I have to enjoy them.

PART I
A Wild Beginning

INTRODUCTION

"Either write something worth reading,
or do something worth writing about."
—BENJAMIN FRANKLIN

This is a story about inspiration. It's a story about family, faith, perseverance, and tenacity. This story is about a girl and her pony and the sport of endurance riding, but mostly it's about overcoming challenges and opening ourselves up to failure in the hope that we will grow, learn, and eventually succeed. It's about the human spirit, the Holy Spirit, the fire-in-the-soul kind of spirit that helps us climb mountains and cross rivers, literally and figuratively. This is about the journey we must all take in life—one of highs and lows, successes and failures. This journey just happens to be along a one-hundred-mile historic trail in the Sierra Nevada mountains, the setting for the most famous endurance race in the world. This is a story about Kyla Law and her small but mighty Hackney pony, Flash, and how for one amazing day, in a world dragged down by a worldwide pandemic, they inspired an international community as Flash became the smallest horse to ever finish the one-hundred mile, one-day Western States Trail Ride—the Tevis Cup..

• • •

For those readers unfamiliar with the sport of endurance riding, the concept is simple. It involves one horse and one rider who must travel together over a marked cross-country course of fifty miles or more within a certain time limit. The horse must pass a series of vet checks to make sure it is fit to continue. Rides are sanctioned by an organization that approves the course and the mileage, sets the rules, and records the results. The rules are in place to protect the safety of the horse, and vets are trained to monitor the equine athletes before, during, and after a ride to make sure they're not under any undue stress. The safety of the rider is secondary!

Riders come in all shapes, sizes, colors, and ages, just like their horses. When endurance riders talk of race, it is simply in the context of an event—one that is open to people everywhere. While finances are always a limiting factor in life, endurance riding can be done on a very low budget—or a very high one—and when we look at the ride results it's apparent that a person's financial status, and status in life, don't appear to matter. Endurance riding offers a level playing field for all participants, where a rescue horse in used tack and brought to the ride in someone else's trailer has as good a chance of competing just as successfully as the high-dollar horse pulled to the ride behind a $300,000 motor home.

I discovered endurance riding in the early 2000s, and it was love at first ride. Actually, my first ride was rather painful and I swore I would never do it again, but I found myself signing up for the next ride a couple of weeks later! I fell in love with the adventure, the sense of community, and the chance to spend hours enjoying the beauty of nature while bonding with the horse beneath me. Somewhere along the way, I heard of the Tevis Cup and read a few books about its history and the challenges of that particular trail. I found it fascinating. I read of a trail that holds people captive. She steals and she teaches, she chews us up and spits us out a changed person, intoxicated by her beauty and the moments of ecstasy she has given us. We feel as if we have touched heaven. She has witnessed the history of humankind in this part of California, allowing us to cross her mountains for hundreds of years. But she has exacted a price.

The Tevis Cup began in 1955 when an Auburn businessman by the name of Wendell Robie took up the challenge to ride one hundred miles in one day on a bet and thereby started an annual event that inspired the sport of endurance riding across the world. The route he chose was the Western States Trail, part of the historic Emigrant Trail from Carson City to Sacramento, used by those crossing the mountains during the days of the California gold rush. The sport has evolved from the times of Wendell Robie. Organizations now sanction the rides and record the ride results, as well as offer mentorships and education.

Horses are the strongest and the most fragile of creatures. In them we find something that mirrors our own souls, and by riding them we find a freedom not often felt in these modern times. Endurance is an addiction, a passion, and a curse. Once hooked, it's hard to let go. We crave the camaraderie of ride camp and the solitude of the trail. Endurance riding offers a microcosm of life. It makes us better. It changes us and it gives us perspective.

I first met Kyla and the Law family at the awards ceremony of the 2021 Tevis Cup. Earlier that morning, my husband and I had wandered the barns at the Gold Country Fairgrounds, just steps from the finish line where only hours before the horse and rider teams had emerged from one hundred miles of trail. Some of the horses were sleeping, hips cocked, having eaten and drunk their fill, and I wondered whether they understood the enormity of what they had just accomplished. I looked at their hooves and wondered exactly how many steps they had taken to cover the hundred miles they had traveled that day.

My husband smiled as he spotted a tiny black pony munching away on a bag of hay almost as big as he was. A very tall horse was standing in the stall next to the pony, his head hanging over the divider as he watched the pony eating beneath him. He had a handsome face, a kind eye. Neither horse looked particularly tired. They were alert, the pony pointedly ignoring us as he kept on eating. I had been following the Facebook page called The Adventures of Flash, the Hackney Pony for a few months now, so I knew who this famous duo was. My husband and I grinned, just like everyone does when they see Flash, and exclaimed about how much smaller he looks in person than in his videos. He was short and lean, and had a mischievous and independent air about him. He had no interest in the strangers standing there admiring him, and there was not one iota of fear in the pony's demeanor. We admired the feisty little pony and his handsome friend who were so obviously attached to each other. No one else was

5

around, and I found myself wondering what Flash's story was; where he had come from, how the girl riding him had felt about her Tevis journey.

We went to the award ceremony but had to leave early, as we had another commitment later that evening in Reno. We stayed long enough to see the top ten horses paraded through an aisle behind the tables where the award banquet is held every year, and then led forward individually to receive a round of applause from a tired but enthusiastic audience. We had watched those same horses earlier as they had been shown for the prestigious Haggin Cup, given to the horse deemed to be in the most superior physical condition of the first ten horses to cross the finish line.

As I sat there, taking it all in, I spotted a young girl in jeans and a white top. She was slim, her dark blonde hair falling well past her shoulders, braces on her teeth, and a pep in her step that only the young have after finishing a one-hundred-mile endurance ride just hours before. I knew it must be Kyla Law. I wanted to go and congratulate her, but she was making her way to one of the tables and greeting those who I assumed were her family. Her mother was dressed in jeans and a blue T-shirt, smiling and talking with her parents, who were obviously excited to be at the awards. They all looked relaxed and happy, and it was hard to believe they had either ridden or crewed a one-hundred-mile ride only hours earlier.

The awards began, and soon the junior riders were called across the stage and given a chance to speak. Kyla said a few words, thanking her mother and her pony, and looking a little awkward at the applause she received. Kyla had been chosen to hand out flowers to all the finishers that would cross the stage that day, and before long her mother was there, smiling from ear to ear and posing with her daughter for a photograph. She had a look of pride that only a parent can truly understand. Her joy was as much for her daughter's accomplishments as her own.

My husband and I had to leave then, and we said our good-byes and headed out to our car. But I couldn't shake the thought that there was a story there somewhere, and I was itching to find out more. The next day I contacted Kyla's mom, Natalie, and asked her if she would be interested in allowing me to work with Kyla on a book. They were on the long drive back to Utah, and with Natalie's consent I found myself exchanging emails with Kyla throughout their drive.

Natalie invited my husband and me to Utah to meet the family, and we arrived not quite sure what to expect. I knew they were members of The Church of Jesus Christ of Latter-day Saints and whatever pre-conceptions I had about them—a quiet, church-going type of family—quickly evaporated.

How do I describe the Laws? By the end of our few days together, I adored the whole family. They were loud, effusive, and had no concern about their own safety (judging by the way they threw themselves from great heights into their backyard pool). They also teased each other mercilessly, and the fact that there were two strangers in their midst didn't change their personalities one bit. You either accepted them as they were, or you didn't. It was also obvious they were a family united in a strong faith. It surrounded them like a gentle light, and within it they shone.

Kyla had been quiet and withdrawn, obviously unable to get a word in edgewise with the louder personalities of her three siblings taking over the conversation, but once we were alone she came to life, and I found myself liking this young lady immensely. She was happy to talk about her life and her experiences. She was honest about the years of bullying she experienced, still ongoing despite all she had achieved. She spoke of her fears and the challenges Flash had presented. Her love for him emanated with every word. She had no idea of the magnitude of what they had achieved by completing the Tevis Cup, although she had finally been allowed to see the social media explosion that had occurred after their finish was announced. For Kyla, it had started as just another ride, important only because she had known that it would be her last with her beloved pony.

The weekend went by quickly. Natalie and Kyla took us riding in a beautiful canyon, and I got to see Flash running wild among the red rocks. I learned a little about his personality and saw him in his element, running free on the trails and adored by a fan club of random hikers whose paths we crossed and who couldn't get enough of the "cute little baby horse!" It was hard to believe that this confident, spicy, adorable, opinionated bit of horseflesh could ever have been the trembling, terrified pony that Kyla had first met.

I also learned that weekend how important faith was to the Law family and how Kyla's journey with Flash had been a parallel journey in her search to strengthen that faith. From nine years old, when she first met Flash, to thirteen, when she did the Tevis Cup, she'd had to navigate a series of challenges that required leaning on her faith and on the foundation her parents and The Church of Jesus Christ of Latter-day Saints had given her. And yet, Kyla had felt she was still lacking in her ability to truly connect with the Holy Spirit. It was only after she experienced the challenges of the Tevis trail that she found a new confidence in her faith and in her connection to God.

To be able to tell this story in its entirety, I worked closely with Natalie and Kyla over the next several months, piecing together their memories and looking at photographs and videos that told their story. I also interviewed others who had either been a part of, or witnessed, Kyla and Flash's transformation: Shelah Wetter, the trainer in Washington State who sold Flash to Kyla and remains a close family friend; Kacey Oar, who knew the family well and crewed for them at Tevis; Dave "The Duck" Nicholson, who has a decades-long history with endurance and whose rides offered Natalie and Kyla some of their most important training miles for Tevis; and Chuck Stalley, race director for the Tevis Cup, who welcomed Kyla and Flash and watched with anticipation as the duo took on the Tevis trail that year. I also interviewed Molly Pearson and Lindsey Fisher, who rode parts of the trail with Natalie and Kyla, and whose testimony added valuable insight into both the Laws' experience and Flash's antics on the trail!

People were very generous of their time, each one extremely happy this story would be told. They admired the grit and determination Kyla had shown, and no one could help falling in love with the pony who seemed to think he was invincible. Their journey spans four years of blood, sweat, and tears. Four years of a search to be closer to God and an appreciation for the beauty of His earth that is amplified from the back of a horse, even a short one! This is the story of Kyla and Flash and their race against time.

PROLOGUE

*"Difficult and meaningful will always bring more
satisfaction than easy and meaningless."*
—MAXIME LAGACÉ

It was dark now, and the trail was pitch black ahead of them. This was the part that thirteen-year-old Kyla Law had dreaded the most. She hadn't been worried about the one hundred miles of historic trail she was taking on that day, or even the overbearing heat of the infamous canyons. She had already battled through thick, smoke-filled pockets of air from the raging wildfires in the distance, the smokey mist creeping into her and her pony's lungs and making it difficult to breathe at times. And she had survived the dreaded five a.m. start where 133 of the fittest horses in the United States waited anxiously to begin the toughest endurance ride in the world—their hooves beating restlessly and repeatedly against the California dirt in anticipation of the adventure ahead. They were now seventy miles into the ride with no daylight left to burn, and for Kyla Law, riding the smallest equine to ever compete in the famous Western States one-hundred-mile, one-day ride, it was the darkness that threatened to derail hers and Flash's effort to conquer the trail.

Up ahead, her mother, Natalie, riding a 16'3" hand Saddlebred named Brave, turned around and squinted into the darkness, trying to make out the shape of her daughter and the tiny pony she sat astride.

"Are you okay, Kyla?" she called out.

"I think so," came the tentative reply.

Gone was the laughing, joking young girl from earlier in the day, the one who had been happily munching on Nabisco Goldfish crackers as she'd expertly maneuvered her pony through a trail that had weaved and zigzagged through the pine forests, eventually dropping into the deepest of canyons, the heat engulfing them the farther they descended. Now Kyla hung tightly onto the front of her pony's saddle for dear life, unable to see where he was stepping or how close he was to the edge of a trail that cut into the sides of the cliff and which seemed to be pulling her constantly toward the edge like a magnet.

Natalie knew of her daughter's fears. They had talked about it before the ride, and Natalie reminded her again of what they had discussed.

"Flash can see the trail better than you can, Kyla!" she called back. "Trust him! Relax! Let him do his job. You know that he won't let you down. You need to have faith. You can do this!"

Faith. The word seeped into Kyla's brain and took hold. She had been raised in The Church of Jesus Christ of Latter-day Saints, and her faith was central to everything she did. She had prayed the night before that she and Flash would finish this race, and she had prayed at various points along the way, gratitude flooding her for the extraordinary experience she and her pony, along with her mother and Brave, had been able to enjoy that day. Now it was time to let go of her fear and put her faith in God and in this amazing creature that He had brought into her life. Faith and the comfort and familiarity of prayer could help her overcome this, the greatest of her challenges.

She also knew that her mom was right. Flash would take care of her as they traversed the final thirty miles of the race, partly because he loved her and partly because in his mind there was nothing he couldn't do. He and Kyla had come through so much together already. For Flash, this was a joyride in the dark. He was a mountain goat, his tiny hooves moving confidently over the ground as if he had been born to do this.

Kyla felt herself relax. In the darkness she was even more aware of Flash's movements beneath her. After fifteen hours in the saddle already today, and years of sitting astride this tiny bundle of attitude, Kyla knew this pony better than anyone. Flash was her best friend, and after everything they had been through together, Kyla knew he would give everything he had to get them both safely to Auburn. The cutoff times at each vet check were always in the back of their minds, pushing them forward, constantly threatening their chance to finish within the twenty-four-hour time limit. For Flash and Kyla, it had been a race against time to even reach the start of Tevis as Kyla had continued to grow, her legs now hanging well below the pony's belly.

Kyla heard the muted hoofbeats of the horses ahead and behind her, and it reminded her that she was traveling on sacred ground. Many others had battled their own demons on this very trail to win that coveted silver belt buckle. Kyla would overcome whatever was up ahead because she knew it was a miracle they were even here.

Natalie was leading the train of horses down the mountain trail that precariously hugged the edge of the cliff face, the Middle Fork of the American River flowing through the curves of the canyon below. Brave had found his groove. He set a steady pace, slowing down over rocks that could bruise the soles of the horses' feet, and speeding up when the trail stretched out ahead. Natalie had found her groove as well and was enjoying the feeling of gliding through the night, the full moon occasionally breaking through the trees and giving her a glimpse of where her horse was taking her. Never hurry, never tarry. The wise words of Kathie Perry from the ride meeting the day before kept repeating in her head. Constant forward motion—that's what they needed to do, each stride bringing them closer to the finish line.

Natalie knew that she was blessed to be experiencing this with her daughter. Together, they were creating a feast of memories that would last a lifetime, not only because they were riding together but because if Kyla and Flash finished, they would earn a place in Tevis Cup history with Flash being the smallest horse to ever complete the one-hundred-mile course. Natalie didn't dwell on this. There were far more pressing issues at hand, and right now, her main concern was hoping her daughter wasn't about to panic in the darkness and jeopardize their ride. She glanced behind her again just as the moonlight broke through the trees, offering Natalie a moment she knew she would never forget. Kyla's eyes shone brightly as she sat up tall in the saddle. Somehow, somewhere she had found the strength she needed to overcome her fear of the darkness, just like she had overcome everything else that day. She gave her mother a brief smile, a smile that said, *I'm fine. I've got this. Flash and I have got this together.*

Natalie turned back to face the trail ahead. She knew that Kyla would have leaned on her faith in this moment. But who would have thought, she mused as Brave swept downward toward the Francisco's vet check, that the scared, wild pony that Kyla met four years ago would be the one to give her the courage she needed now, in this moment, to conquer the Tevis trail.

CHAPTER 1

An Uncertain Future

"The finish line is for the ego, the journey is for the soul."
—PATTI GONIA

The pony stood in the back of the pen shaking with fear. His dark eyes flicked back and forth nervously as he watched the people on the other side of the stall door. He didn't trust them. He never had. He wanted to be left alone, as he had been for so many years, other than the occasional handling to trim his feet or give him his annual vaccines, and he had fought against those ministrations like a Mustang just captured off the range.

Flash knew he had nowhere to run, and he felt trapped and scared. His tail was tucked between his legs. His entire body trembled. He wanted nothing to do with the people standing there looking at him, especially the shorter ones who tended to squeal and make all types of noises and movements he wasn't used to. The pony was small and black; small even for a Hackney pony, as if he were the runt of a litter. His body was of a finer build than the stocky little ponies often used to carry small children around. His was more the body of an athlete, or it would have been had he not spent the last few years getting fat and lazy in that Oregon pasture. His name was Piece of Perfection, and his future was uncertain.

Ponies are generally purchased by parents or riding school instructors, neither of whom are looking for a very small and mostly feral pony that has never been ridden. They are looking for something cute and safe, a babysitter to carry their precious child around as they learn the basics of being a rider. To add to the challenge, there are few adults small enough to ride an 11'2" pony in order to train it, and very few children advanced enough in their riding skills to do the job, especially when faced with a feral pony with an aversion to human contact.

Flash was one of those ponies that had fallen between the cracks. He had been left to his own devices for too long. His current owner recognized that, at eight years old, if Flash was going to have any hope for a full life, he needed to be sold to someone who could give him a better chance. Although he was wild, he was surely cute enough to attract someone's attention. It was time for the pony to move on.

• • •

Shelah Wetter was a horse trainer and riding instructor who had grown up on a horse breeding farm in Deer Park, Washington. Her mother, Pam Heiman, had been breeding American Saddlebreds since before Shelah was born, and Shelah had grown up learning about the old-school bloodlines her mother selectively bred. By the time she was five years old, Shelah was traveling with her mother up and down the west coast of America showing their home-bred Saddlebred horses, and by age eleven, she was taking on clients of her own. Shelah wanted to continue her mother's breeding program and showcase the Saddlebred as America's horse, bred to carry people for long hours in the saddle comfortably, with a friendly and amenable disposition.

As Shelah grew, the horses remained a primary focus in her life. But a bad accident derailed her plans in 2011, and Shelah began teaching more and showing less. She heard about a sport called endurance riding and decided to test her Saddlebreds in the sport to prove their versatility outside of the show ring.

Shelah Wetter met Natalie Law when Natalie bought a Saddlebred mare from a client of Shelah's. From that initial meeting the two women became great friends, and a couple of years later, Natalie began taking her children to Shelah's stables for riding lessons. Shelah remembers fondly that the children were mostly feral, and while one would be having a lesson, the others would be running wild, left to their own devices and occasionally getting left behind when Natalie tried to gather up her brood to leave. One of the games the children would play was to climb on top of the hayrack of Shelah's horse trailer and launch themselves into the piles of snow that had accumulated during the worst winter months. They also loved to play in what Shelah refers to as the poop swamp, happily romping through the horse dung until it was time to load back into the car for home. Over the years, Shelah became a huge part of the Law family's life, and they became a huge part of hers.

Through Shelah, Natalie was introduced to the sport of endurance riding. Endurance riding fit Natalie's personality and goals perfectly. She loved being on the back of a horse exploring the natural beauty of God's earth, and she appreciated the challenges that riding over long distances presented. Although endurance is a sport dominated by the Arabian horse, the Saddlebred breed had a natural athleticism that made them a strong contender on the trails.

Shelah had bought her first Hackney pony when she was nine years old. She loved the high action of the Hackney pony and the unique attitude of the breed, which was known for possessing great stamina and being tenacious and brave. They also have big, friendly personalities, making them popular as both show and companion animals. Over the years Shelah owned several of these ponies, and in 2017 she decided to look for a retired Hackney show pony that could be used to give lessons to her students.

Shelah freely admits that she buys horses like other women buy shoes. She had heard of a pony belonging to a lady she knew whose father had once run a successful Hackney breeding program. The program had shut down, and Flash had been put out to pasture with hardly any handling for several years. Flash was likely introduced to pulling a cart in his early years, and possibly the five-inch scar on his rump was the result of a cart accident. Shelah didn't really know all the details of his life prior to coming to Blue Haven Stables, but when she saw a photograph of the tiny pony, she immediately told the seller to load him up and send him over. They organized a shipper who delivered Flash to Shelah in Washington State in the middle of a terrible snowstorm, and both the pony and the shipper arrived wild-eyed and extremely annoyed. Flash was morbidly obese and feral, and Shelah figured she had her work cut out for her with this one.

Once Shelah got him home, she wasn't sure what to do with him next. He was smaller than most Hackney ponies, who tend to range between twelve and fourteen hands. Flash, fully grown, stood at just 11'2" hands (46 inches at his shoulder, to be precise). Conformationally, he was exactly the way a Hackney pony should be, with a small head, powerful shoulders, a compact back, and a slight frame. Well, he would be, if he weren't carrying so much extra weight. He was obviously too small for her to ride, and there was no way she was going to get him hooked to a cart any time soon without causing them both irreparable harm.

Flash was scared of everything, but most especially small children and things that were behind him. If a small child was behind him, all hell would break loose. Fear made Flash unpredictable and explosive, but Shelah felt that this small and terrified creature had more to offer than met the eye. It was a gut feeling. There was something about the way he moved, the look in his eye once you saw beyond the fear, and even a sense of destiny that surrounded the tiny creature. He looked like a delicate child's toy, but one filled with dynamite and party poppers.

"What on earth am I going to do with you?" Shelah would say as she stared at Flash, shaking her head slowly. Shelah needed to give Flash a job, and to do that she needed someone who could help her handle and eventually ride him. What Flash needed was a human as small of stature as he was. Someone who could ride a feral pony but who would first take the time to befriend him and bring him out of his shell. He needed a person of his own to bond with so he could overcome his fear and learn how to trust. Shelah realized she already knew the perfect child for the job. She had been giving lessons to Kyla Law for many years, and the girl was a natural when it came to horses. She could stick to a horse like gum to the underside of a shoe, but she also had a gentle and sweet spirit that would make any animal feel at ease. If Kyla was up to the task, she could be the person to give Flash the chance of a productive life. Shelah smiled to herself. Kyla and Flash would be a perfect match, and the sooner she could get the two of them together, the better.

CHAPTER 2

Building a Bond

"It always seems impossible until it is done."
—NELSON MANDELA

Kyla Law had been taking lessons from Shelah since she was six years old. She had graduated from the dullest lesson horse Shelah owned to being able to ride any horse that Shelah threw her on. Kyla was small for her nine years—slight of build, with light bones, long limbs, and a sweet but bookish kind of face. She wore blue-framed glasses, and her dark blonde hair hung straight past her shoulders. Her manner was reserved around strangers, but no middle child of a rambunctious family survived without having great self-preservation skills. Kyla had guts. The kind of guts a person would need to take on a wild pony with a whole bunch of issues. Plus, she could clamber onto any horse and cling to it like a spider monkey.

Shelah was excited to introduce the idea of riding Flash to the young girl. She had a feeling this could be the beginning of something special for them both.

Shelah had owned Flash for three months but had not had time to do more than the basics with him. If she approached him carefully, he could be caught and haltered, and he would stand long enough to have his hooves trimmed for the farrier. Sort of. She tried to give him a vaccination shot once, and the pony had a complete meltdown.

While he was improving physically, mentally he was a mess. The slightest thing could set him off, and Shelah knew that if he didn't start learning to trust and accept human contact soon, his future was bleak. Luckily, he had more personality than any pony Shelah had ever met. She was sure that if Kyla would take the time to work with him, and stick with him through all his shenanigans, she would be rewarded with his loyalty and trust. Eventually.

Kyla had seen Flash before. In order to help get him used to children, Shelah had often pinned the pony into the corner of a stall and asked the Law kids to come in to pet him. For Flash, with his inborn fear of children, this was a form of absolute torture, and Shelah quickly realized that he would do better bonding with just one person of his own. When Kyla first approached Flash's stall, knowing this time she had the chance to be his one special person, she looked at him differently; not just as Shelah's wild pony, but as a pony she would have the chance to befriend, if he would allow it.

Kyla's eyes were as curious as those of the pony that stared back at her. Shelah stood next to Kyla and watched the girl's face go through a series of emotions as she stared at the pony before her. This was going to be a huge undertaking and Kyla knew it. She appreciated Shelah's confidence in her, but she had serious doubts about her ability to help him, especially when she saw the way he stared back at her—his eyes full of fear and his body trembling.

Shelah encouraged Kyla to step closer.

"Do you think he'll like me?" Kyla asked. She asked herself this question with everyone she met now. She hadn't even realized she'd asked it out loud until Shelah answered.

"What's not to like?"

Kyla was a little socially insecure herself and often felt like an outsider, not fully accepted at school and overshadowed by the stronger personalities in her family. She may have instinctively known what Flash needed, recognizing a kindred spirit. When Kyla was quiet, the pony calmed down and stared at her from the back of his pen, curious but wary of the small human. But when Kyla spoke, he once again shook in fear, his body trembling from a deep-seated terror he had acquired at some point in his life.

"Why are you so scared?" Kyla asked him quietly. "I would never hurt you!"

Shelah's heart melted watching the two interact for the first time. She had known that Kyla had the ability to ride Flash, but she also knew it would take a sensitive soul to understand the terrified pony standing before them. Kyla had grit *and* compassion, the perfect recipe to break down the pony's walls and teach him how to trust.

Standing there that day, neither Kyla, Flash, nor Shelah Wetter knew this was the first moment of a partnership that would make history. All Kyla knew was that it was *her* job to somehow teach this little pony that he didn't need to be afraid, even if sometimes it was difficult to remind herself of the same thing. This was a partnership that would be forged from desire, persistence, and effort. And thank goodness Flash was cute, because sometimes that was all he would have going for him in their months ahead.

• • •

At nine years old, Kyla was the second oldest child of four. She had an older brother, Gabe, and two younger sisters, Emma and Layla. Their parents, Adam and Natalie Law, had rooted their family in a solid foundation within The Church of Jesus Christ of Latter-day Saints. They gave their children the freedom to explore the world around them and learn from their own mistakes. This upbringing, particularly being one of four outgoing siblings, made Kyla tough in ways that belied her somewhat fragile appearance.

Natalie Law was a fun-loving mother with a passion for life and a passion for all animals, but for horses in particular. Adam worked in medical sales and was gone three to five days every week, leaving Natalie to run a busy household in his absence. With four children, a hard-working husband, three horses, two dogs, a llama, a pig, some goats, two alpacas, and a couple of barn cats, Natalie's life was just a little busy. When Shelah told Natalie that she wanted Kyla to help train Flash, Natalie had to think carefully about how she could fit the extra time Kyla would need to be at the stables into an already crowded schedule. When she saw how enthusiastic Kyla was about working with the pony, she figured she could drop Kyla off twice a week to work with Flash by herself, or with Shelah. Then she would stay there for one session a week with her daughter so she could see the progress, or lack thereof, in the pony's training.

Kyla had never been faced with a challenge like Flash. The horses she had been around in the past had been used to human touch and well-integrated into a life of domesticity. Even Shelah called the pony "terrible" and "a little hellion." Kyla knew that to begin connecting with Flash she would need to approach him on his own terms. She would have to learn how to quiet herself and her emotions around the pony because if she raised her voice, or made any sudden movements, he would become instantly suspicious and fearful, running as far away from her as he could get. Those first few weeks of their training, Kyla spent as many hours with him as possible, just standing or sitting in his pen and allowing him to become familiar with her quiet presence.

Offering Flash a treat, Kyla learned, could draw him closer to her. She would enter his stall, her hand outstretched, holding a carrot or a few oats to tempt him. Before long he was edging toward her, his tiny hooves tentative, ready to take flight at any moment. Once he got close enough, his little body still a safe distance away, he would stretch his neck as far as it would go, extending his muzzle to her outstretched palm. Then he would grab whatever she was offering and immediately retreat to where he had started, pleased with himself for outsmarting this small human and stealing her food. This was an early sign of the pony's capacity for playing games, always wanting to win and outsmart his opponent, whether human or horse.

After a month of spending time together this way, the day finally came. Kyla reached out to him and Flash stayed where he was, letting her hand rest on his neck. She could hardly believe it. She focused on breathing slowly and staying calm, but in her mind she was screaming, *I did it! He finally let me touch him!*

After that first moment of acceptance, it only took a week before Flash would stand quietly as Kyla ran her hands over his body, as long as she was completely silent and stayed away from his ears and his rump. Kyla avoided his five-inch scar to the right of his tail, learning that it was an area where Flash would never feel comfortable being touched, even years later.

While Flash's scars from his past showed on the outside, Kyla's were hidden on the inside, but the girl knew they shared some of the same pain. If they were to develop trust between them, it would be a game of give and take. She allowed Flash his few quirky habits as long as they made progress overall. She loved finally getting close enough to Flash to touch and smell him.

There's a saying that the outside of a horse is good for the inside of a man. Kyla found that there's also something about the smell and the steady breath of a pony that's good for healing the heart of a little girl.

Two months into his training, Flash would allow Kyla to groom him, and she spent hours and hours doing this, first in complete silence, but later talking to him in hushed tones, reassuring him that everything was okay and that he was safe with her. Kyla's consistency and ability to keep going were finally paying off, even though some days it seemed as if they were taking a step backward instead of forward. Although he never liked it, with Shelah's help Kyla was now able to slip a halter over Flash's head, and in addition to the hours of grooming, she could finally take the pony for walks around the stables.

He was getting used to her voice, and she would tell him everything—how her day went in school and what her life was like. How her one sister, Emma, would tease her, while the other sister, Layla, would sneak into her room and play with her toys or steal her candy. "We're still close, though," Kyla told him. "I think they actually look up to me like I do with Gabe. He really does look out for me at school when the kids are being mean." Flash understood Kyla. She could feel it.

Kyla could not remember a time at school when she hadn't felt bullied. At first it had been subtle, a comment here and there that surprised her with its ability to make her feel uncomfortable, but then the bullying became less subtle and more consistent. Finally, its incessant pitch made Kyla withdraw into a protective shell, trying to make herself disappear so her classmates would forget she was even there. To those who didn't know her she appeared shy and quiet, but to her family, and to her mother especially, the change in her was becoming apparent. Natalie desperately tried to figure out what she could do to help. Bullying was destroying Kyla's confidence bit by bit, day by day, until her entire world altered, a ghastly shadow of doubt following her wherever she went. Between classes Kyla walked the corridors with her eyes cast down and an expectation of disappointment that wouldn't go away.

For Kyla, having something besides the bullying to focus on, such as training a wild pony, was a needed relief. It gave her a distraction, and with each tiny step that she and Flash took together, her sense of accomplishment grew and a little piece of her self-confidence returned. Somehow, the pair were finding exactly what they needed in each other. Flash had found a human he could trust, while Kyla had found a best friend who was always willing to listen to her secrets. Kyla's time with Flash had become the best part of her day. From what she knew of God's hand, this seemed like His doing, offering girl and pony a chance to grow together beyond anything they could have been apart.

• • •

Flash's back was short enough that Kyla could lean over it, gradually adding more weight as the pony became comfortable with the feel of her. For any horse, wild or domestic, having someone on their back puts them at their most vulnerable. This was the area where a mountain lion would leap on top of them from a rock formation as they went by, and the fear was so deeply ingrained into their ancient memory that even a horse bred in captivity displays the same fear as one born in the wild.

Whenever Flash became nervous, Kyla would simply back off, rubbing and scratching his neck in the places she knew he liked the most until he was calm and she could try again. The day came when Kyla was confident that Flash was ready to allow her on his back. With both her mom and Shelah present, Kyla led Flash over to the cross ties and clipped his halter securely onto each side. This would limit how far he could go in any direction so Kyla would be safe from an all-out explosion that could harm both of them. She hoped she had done enough groundwork that this would be a pleasant experience for the pony, and not one that would threaten the bonds of trust they had so carefully been building.

"Just approach him slowly but confidently," Shelah advised. "Don't make a big deal out of it or he'll become suspicious."

Kyla gently placed her leg over Flash's back and slid onto him, finally straddling the little pony. He shifted beneath her, his mind trying to decipher what was going on, but he stayed calm. For the first time, he was allowing someone in this vulnerable place, and all because of the many hours Kyla had spent with him over the past couple of months building their friendship. Flash shifted his weight again, trying to get a feel for this new experience. He didn't know it, but this was an important moment in their history together. Kyla saw the view between Flash's ears, and it was a sight that she would become very familiar with over the next few years.

She smiled at Shelah. "Look how good he's being!" she said seconds before he dumped her on the ground.

But from this moment on they progressed further and faster. With Shelah's help, Kyla was able to put a saddle on Flash's back and get him used to the feel of a bit in his mouth. After the enormous amount of time it had taken to initially gain his trust, Flash now progressed quickly. It wasn't long before Kyla could ride him in the large indoor arena at Shelah's facility, so long as Shelah had him on a lead line or was ponying him off the back of her horse. Flash learned how to carry a rider to decipher how Kyla was communicating with him through the reins, her seat, and her legs.

He was smart and learned quickly, but Flash was not a placid, cooperative pony. He tested his rider at every opportunity, and it was fortunate that Kyla was not easily intimidated by his fiery attitude. After a few weeks Shelah started putting Flash on a lunge line, having Kyla ride around her in circles, teaching Flash how to balance under Kyla's weight on a circle. He became more accustomed to being ridden, but it was a tenuous partnership between him and Kyla. Sometimes she was in charge, but just as often Flash would think he got to make the decisions.

Flash finally settled down beneath her so long as Kyla was absolutely silent. If she spoke, he exploded. He wouldn't buck or rear, but he would bolt—fast. He had speed like Shelah had never seen in a pony, and Kyla came off him repeatedly, often resulting in bruises or a bloody nose. But Kyla didn't give up, although she may have been tempted to if Flash hadn't been so cute. More than that, though, Kyla understood that his behavioral issues came from fear. He wasn't just misbehaving—not most of the time anyway. She knew that to get the most out of their relationship, he was going to need to trust her, and she him.

Being unable to talk while on his back was obviously not acceptable, so Shelah had to devise a plan to help Flash get over whatever it was about Kyla talking that set him off.

"Today, when you are on him, I want you to start saying the alphabet in a whisper. Once you feel him relax, start singing it softly. Gradually get louder, but if you feel him tense up under you, get quieter again. Let's see how he deals with that."

Kyla said nothing, but Shelah could easily decipher her look: *Sure, easy for you to say, since you're not the one on his back!* But she mounted and did exactly as Shelah had asked.

Although it took a while, this method seemed to work, and gradually the pony accepted not only the *feel* of Kyla on his back but also the *sound* of her as well. He made the connection that the girl who spoke to him on the ground was the same girl speaking to him from his back, and once that clicked, it made riding him a lot less tricky.

Kyla was proud of their progress. It had taken three months to get this far, but with Shelah there to help and advise her, Kyla was beginning to get comfortable riding Flash. Even though she had sometimes doubted her ability to help him overcome his fear, Kyla was glad to have found a partner in Flash. Through steady and consistent work, their progress showed. Kyla spent as much time just being with him and talking to him as she did training him. She called him her secret keeper. She could talk to Flash about anything, and once he lost his fear of her voice, he appeared to welcome it, knowing that he was needed as well as loved. Somehow, this tiny being had managed to crawl his way into her heart, and Kyla could not imagine a life without him. He had become her best friend, her confidant. She thanked God for putting Flash into her life just when she had so desperately needed something to love that could love her back. She couldn't imagine ever having to say goodbye to her precious pony, but unfortunately, it seemed as though she was going to have to learn. Kyla was used to disappointment, but she wasn't sure how to handle what happened next.

CHAPTER 3

Goodbye Copper, Hello Flash!

"Be yourself, everyone else is already taken."

—OSCAR WILDE

The Laws were getting ready to move. Natalie's parents had settled in Southern Utah among the dramatic red rock cliffs and high desert just north of St. George. Adam Law had lived there before. It took little to convince themselves this was the place where they needed to make their home and continue raising their family. Among the many reasons for the move, they felt that a fresh start for Kyla, away from the increasing problems at school, would be a positive thing.

Kyla was a good student, but for some reason she was having a hard time fitting in with her peers. Maybe because she was raised in The Church of Jesus Christ of Latter-day Saints, or maybe because she was small for her age and lacked confidence. For whatever reason, Kyla drew the attention of those children who fed off the insecurities of others and they made her school days unbearable. Being kind and sensitive herself, Kyla couldn't understand why her schoolmates would go out of their way to make her feel bad. Sometimes their meanness was subtle, inviting Kyla to meet up somewhere then leaving without her. Sometimes it was less subtle. She would hear loud whispers as she walked past the kids in the hallways or playground. Kyla despaired not knowing what she had done to attract this negativity. She would lay in bed at night worrying about what would happen the next day—whether the bullying would become physical, the constant question circling, *why me?* She continued to withdraw from the social aspect of school and find more comfort in the company of her animals instead.

Natalie was brokenhearted at her daughter's suffering. She felt helpless and angry in equal measure. She went to the school and complained to both Kyla's teachers and the principal. This was not a short-term thing. It had been going on since kindergarten, and if it hadn't been for her best friend, Kylie, Kyla might have simply refused to go to school. As it was, she dreaded getting up in the mornings. Her confidence was at an all-time low, and her parents could see that she was carrying the pain of it around constantly. It was affecting the person she was becoming. Despite nightly prayer, which offered Kyla some comfort, the bullying continued, and Natalie grew tired of seeing her daughter unhappy.

"Not everyone that you meet in life will like you, Kyla. It will usually have more to do with them not liking themselves or trying to show off in front of their friends than anything you've done," Natalie told her daughter one evening.

"I guess I know that," Kyla replied. "But there's a difference between someone not liking you and leaving you alone, and someone not liking you and going out of their way to be mean."

Kyla would repeatedly fall prey to a fake overture of friendship, only to have her heart broken once again as those same kids campaigned against her behind her back.

Natalie felt that her attempts to rectify the situation with the school fell on deaf ears. When it became obvious that they weren't going to do anything to help their daughter, Natalie and Adam determined that their best option was to remove her from the school completely, hoping that the next school they put her in would offer their daughter a better chance of happiness.

• • •

The big move was looming in just a few weeks. Suddenly Kyla had to face the fact that her journey with Flash could be over, and soon—before she would ever be able to see what they could become together.

What would Flash do without her? The thought of being separated after going through so much together was almost too unbearable to consider.

Shelah was also having the same concerns. Who would continue Flash's training now that Kyla would no longer be there? And would it really be fair to separate the two of them now that they had come this far together? Shelah had an idea. She checked with Natalie first and then approached Kyla, who had tied Flash to the hitching post and was grooming his coat and talking away to him as if he were another human.

"It's going to be hard for you to leave that pony," Shelah began. Kyla couldn't even look at her. She hated the thought of losing her best friend, and tears formed in her eyes at the reminder. Soon she wouldn't be able to spend time grooming Flash, let alone whispering her secrets to him.

"But what if you don't have to?" Shelah inquired, putting her hand on Kyla's shoulder and turning the girl toward her.

Kyla looked up, confused at what Shelah had just said.

"I spoke to your mom, Kyla, and if your dad agrees I will sell Flash to you for exactly what I paid for him. Five hundred dollars. Would you like to take him with you to Utah? You'd have to continue to work really hard with him, but I know you could do it!"

"Really? Do you mean it?" Kyla said, not quite believing what she had just heard.

Tears overflowed as she hugged her friend and trainer, and then she immediately turned to hug Flash. She poked her glasses out of the way as she wiped the happy tears from her eyes. She still had to persuade her father, but even the possibility of taking Flash with her seemed too good to be true.

Shelah could feel her own eyes threatening tears in that moment. Then she heard Kyla whisper into Flash's neck, "You might be coming with me, Flash. Wouldn't that be perfect? I love you so much," and Shelah gave up trying to hold the tears back.

• • •

Natalie and Kyla knew that Adam would be the one who needed the most convincing, but like most good men, his weak spot was for the happiness of his wife and children. Kyla had saved for years. Any money she had earned from chores or received for her birthday or Christmas had been diligently stowed away, waiting for just such an occasion as this. If she could persuade her father to allow her to become Flash's owner, she would be able to buy him herself with all the money she had accumulated in her savings.

But Adam was resistant. He hadn't witnessed firsthand the bond that Kyla had built with the pony, so Kyla tried another way. She sat down and wrote her father a letter explaining just how much Flash meant to her, and how she would be responsible for everything the pony ever needed. She told her father how hard she had worked to earn the pony's trust and how, over the past few months, he had become her best friend. She also explained to her father that Flash was the one she told her problems to, cried with, and relied on to make her day better when she'd had a difficult day at school. It would break her heart to lose him now.

What father could say no to that? But Adam still gave Kyla one last challenge to overcome to prove she was ready for horse ownership. Although Kyla had enough money to purchase Flash, it would take everything she had in her savings account to make it happen. Adam's stipulation was that Kyla find enough money to also pay for Flash's health certificate and brand inspection, and to have his teeth floated before they left. Adam wanted to make sure that his daughter appreciated not just the purchase price of a pony but all the other costs that came with horse ownership as well. He waited to see what Kyla would do to overcome this final hurdle to bringing the pony with them on the move.

Kyla was in the habit of stashing any money she earned from odd jobs that she did around the neighborhood in a variety of hiding places in her bedroom since her siblings often snuck into her room uninvited. She enlisted the help of her grandmother, Wynona, and while they packed up her things for the imminent move, they also searched on hands and knees around her room, extracting five- and ten-dollar bills from inside shoes, between the pages of books, and tucked into her clothes drawers. But when she tallied up her findings, she was still about $250 short. Wynona could have helped her, but her son-in-law had insisted that Kyla would learn a much better life lesson if she could figure out a way to do this herself.

Kyla stood up and looked around at all her possessions. She was a young girl, so she didn't have too much in the world worth selling. But in the corner of her room sat her prized corn snake, Copper. Kyla knew that if she sold him, plus his elaborate snake habitat, she might have enough money to close the deal on Flash. While this sounded like a big sacrifice, in truth Copper had bitten her quite badly the week before so the decision was much easier to make, and Copper found himself off to a new home to bite some other poor, unsuspecting child.

Kyla had now added enough money to her stash to make the deal and meet her father's demands. Had she really done it? Had she found a way to bring Flash to Utah with her and not have to say goodbye to the pony who had come to mean so much to her?

It appeared she had.

CHAPTER 4

A Big Deal for a Small Horse

*"The difference between winning and
losing is most often not quitting."*

—WALT DISNEY

It was July 8, two weeks before the big move. Shelah was happy for Kyla and Flash, but she still needed to make the sale official. She filled out a bill of sale and wrote up a contract that would give Kyla full ownership. It was a big day for Kyla. She had never owned a horse of her own, and the fact that she had managed to purchase him herself made the moment even more special.

Flash was brought in to witness the signing of the paperwork, and it seemed as if he understood what was going on as he nudged Kyla's hand in the direction of where she needed to sign. Kyla was overwhelmed—the pony was now officially hers. The responsibility of owning a horse was both a privilege and a huge responsibility. As Kyla smiled for the photographs the adults were taking to commemorate the special occasion of his purchase, her mind was spinning with the gravity of what she had just done. Kyla wanted to do right by him but suddenly realized that both she and Flash would now be training on their own. She would have her mother's help, of course, but Shelah, her riding instructor and friend, and the person who knew Flash best in the world other than herself, would be hundreds of miles away. Kyla hadn't even ridden him outside of the arena yet, or without being on a lead line. The thought of taking over Flash's training without Shelah was daunting.

Natalie had found a western saddle small enough to fit Flash and had bought him a new bright green biothane bridle and reins. At least he now looked the part of a domesticated pony. Flash was still not completely comfortable with the idea of being ridden, but he was beginning to get the idea and he was no longer shaking in fear every time Kyla approached him. In fact, he would now look for Kyla and wait by the gate for her to arrive and take him out. He had slimmed down, and his coat had become shiny and sleek, thanks to the many hours of grooming that Kyla had done to bond with him.

Flash was a stunning pony. His coat was a deep bay, turning to black as it ran down his legs toward his tiny hooves. He had small bands of white above three of those hooves and a tiny white star in the center of his forehead. His mane and tail were black, his tail so thick that it flowed behind him as he moved. He didn't have the very high-stepping action that the Hackney breed is known for, but that would make him a more efficient trail horse, without wasting energy by being too showy in his movement. Shelah knew that if anyone could make Flash into a successful, well-trained pony, it was the Law family.

Before Flash could make the trip, he needed to have a Coggins test, which involved having blood drawn to test for the presence of antibodies to a disease called Equine Infectious Anemia in the horse's blood. If Flash tested positive to the EIA antibodies—a potentially life-threatening disease with no cure or treatment—he would not be authorized to travel. Flash also needed a recorded brand inspection to be able to pass across state lines and enter Utah. It was a credit to all the time Kyla had put into his training that she was able to persuade the pony to stand for the vet to have his blood drawn. He was given a light sedative so his teeth could be checked and have any sharp points filed down to make him as comfortable as possible, both to eat and to take the bit in his mouth for riding. Flash passed his vet exam with flying colors. Each situation he was facing was a large step toward entering the world of domesticity and leaving his feral habits behind.

On the day of the move, Kyla and her family arrived at Shelah's ready to take Flash to his new home. Kyla didn't know how to thank Shelah for giving her this opportunity, so she simply put her arms around Shelah's neck. "Thank you!" Kyla whispered.

That was good enough for Shelah.

"Now don't worry about training him without me," she told Kyla. "I'm just a phone call away. Your mom can send me videos, and you can ask me questions any time you need to, okay? You'll know what you need to do to help him. Just don't get into your own head too much with doubts. And make sure you don't try to train him when you're hungry!" she added, knowing that Kyla was extremely cranky when she hadn't eaten and would be in no frame of mind to deal with the pony's antics. Kyla smiled at that, knowing it was true. Both she and her mom were terrible when they hadn't been fed. Everyone who knew them, knew to stay away or give them food.

Finally, the time came to leave. Shelah and Kyla exchanged a long hug. Shelah was glad that she'd had the foresight to put these two together, especially as she saw them progress over the next few years. Kyla had found a mentor and a friend in Shelah, someone she would never forget and who had been instrumental in bringing her and Flash together. Shelah had also offered Kyla friendship and adult guidance outside of her immediate family at a time when Kyla had needed it the most and Kyla would be forever grateful.

Now came the challenge of loading Flash into a three-horse trailer that already had three horses inside. Luckily, trailer loading had never been one of Flash's challenges. For some reason he was always happy to hop into a trailer. Maybe it was his inner sense of adventure that made him ready to see what was at the other end of any journey.

He would be traveling to Utah with three other horses that the Laws owned. Brave, or Mo Motion Jack, was a Saddlebred gelding that Natalie had purchased for Adam from Adam's aunt, hoping she could turn him into the perfect husband horse. Brave was six years old and tall at 16'3" hands.

Dixie was another Saddlebred, bred at Shelah's Blue Haven Stables. She was a dark bay and was the boss mare of the group. Her registered name was Hero's Pzazz, and Natalie had been riding her in endurance riding, recognizing that Dixie had the natural talent and mental attitude to do well in the sport. Once they settled in Utah, Natalie had plans to explore the sport further, as there were organized rides within easy driving distance of their new home. Plus the stunning and rugged trails of that area would allow her to experience the beauty of God's earth from the back of a horse. What could be more perfect?

The third horse in the trailer was a sweet little mare named Willow. Willow was a red dun quarter horse. She was a rare horse, not only in her beauty but also in her sweet nature. She had a kind and generous spirit and loved everyone in the Law family, but especially the children. She and Kyla had an especially close relationship, and before Flash it had been Willow that Kyla had ridden the most. Willow never caused problems with the other horses and was everyone's friend in the barn. It was Willow who babysat Flash on the sixteen-hour journey from Spokane, Washington, to Leeds, Utah. They stood nose to tail, and it was not hard to imagine Willow explaining to Flash that he had just landed in the best place possible, with a family who would love and care for him for the rest of his days.

• • •

The Law family finally arrived in Utah looking like a cross between *The Grapes of Wrath* and *The Beverly Hillbillies*. They moved into a small rental house and placed the animals at a ranch a few minutes down the road. They were planning to build their dream home and had secured the perfect location tucked back into a red rock canyon adjacent to Natalie's parents.

The animals found themselves in a climate very different than the one they left. Washington State was cool, damp, and green, while Utah was a land of dry, high deserts, and tall, rugged cliffs framed against an almost cloudless sky. Besides the change in climate, the horses found themselves in the strange situation of boarding in a place where they were trapped between a large herd of cows and a busy freeway. The constant honking, air brakes from semi-trucks, and incessant mooing from their new neighbors was not what they were accustomed to. But it would be another year and a half before they moved into their permanent home in a peaceful canyon, and until then they would have to learn to deal with all the changes that had been thrown at them. Natalie figured that it would be a great desensitizing exercise for them all, and time proved her right. Soon Dixie was the only one who still seemed agitated by all the noise and activity. The other horses didn't even bother to raise their heads from their feed if a semi-truck drove within ten feet of them.

The animals were not the only ones who had to adjust to all the changes. For the Law children, the move meant new schools, a new church, and the challenge of making new friends. Being a member of The Church of Jesus Christ of Latter-day Saints meant they had immediate access to families with the same faith and similar values, and having Natalie's parents nearby made the move easier on the whole family. Many of Adam's friends from when he had lived in the area were still around and welcomed them, but like most big life changes, it would take time for the Laws to truly integrate into the local community and feel settled. Adam was starting his own business, and Natalie was not only helping him from home with some of the administrative duties, but she was also settling the children into new schools and making sure that the horses were fed and cared for twice a day. Add the stress of building a new home, and sometimes it seemed as if the move was going on forever.

Both Natalie and Kyla relieved their stress by spending time with the horses, enjoying the familiarity of their smell and the comfort of their warm bodies. Flash's registered name was Piece of Perfection, but Shelah had given him the barn name of Napoleon Dynamite due to his constant explosions. Kyla wanted to rename him and give him a fresh start with his new life as a member of their family. After a few trial names, the name Flash stuck the best. It rolled easily off the tongue, and like a flash of lightning, it also reflected the pony's desire to go fast everywhere he went.

There was one overwhelming challenge, though, and that challenge rolled like a dark cloud over Kyla and Flash's heads the longer they were together. Flash was tiny. He was nine years old and would never grow any larger. He would get fitter and better trained, but he would never grow any taller. Kyla, on the other hand, was now ten years old and seemed to be growing taller every day. Flash's tiny stature meant that Kyla, like all children, would eventually outgrow her prized pony. Kyla felt the pressure to do as much with Flash as she could, knowing they had a finite amount of time together. It was like taking a trip on a train knowing that somewhere up ahead the train would run out of track. The question was, when?

CHAPTER 5

The Fear of Failure

"Everyone you admire was once a beginner."

—JACK BUTCHER

Kyla was still stepping up to the challenge of keeping Flash's training going, even without the direct supervision she was used to from Shelah. Flash was not easy. His mind was as quick as his feet, and without the safety of being on a lead line Kyla wasn't sure exactly how he would react to certain situations. It took persistence, patience, and repetition to get through every quirky thing in the universe that Flash had a problem with. But Kyla rose to the challenge. Working with Flash was not exactly what Kyla would call fun. Many times she doubted her ability to help him, but she did her best and never gave up, despite the many times she ended up on the ground. She became an expert at knowing when to hold on and when to bail, and she was turning into quite the gymnast with her unplanned dismounts.

Natalie was settling into a new routine too. Each morning around seven-thirty she would go to the ranch to feed the horses while the children got themselves ready for school. After school the kids would come with her to ride and help with barn chores. Natalie didn't bother getting dressed before going to the barn in the mornings. She just tucked her pj's into her muck boots and called it good. If there was a bite to the air, she would throw on her Carhartt jacket and begin throwing hay to the waiting horses.

One morning, as she approached the corrals, she noticed there was something wrong with Willow, the sweet little dun mare. There was blood on her face, and blood smeared on her feed tub and smattered throughout her pen. It looked like a murder scene. Natalie climbed into the pen and ran her hands all over Willow, certain she must have a horrific open wound somewhere, but she found nothing. Willow seemed fine and was looking around for her morning feed. There was a lot of dried blood below one of Willow's nostrils, and Natalie assumed that the horse must have suffered a horrific nosebleed. Since she seemed fine now, Natalie went ahead and fed her and the other horses before returning home to get the children off to school. Once she had made the school run, she would call the vet's office to schedule an appointment to have Willow checked. Since they were new to the area, Natalie hadn't established herself as a client with a large animal vet, so when she called the office, she wasn't able to book an appointment for an emergency visit, especially since the emergency seemed to be over. After trying to explain what was going on, she was told that if the horse was eating and drinking, and there was no longer blood flowing from anywhere, Willow was probably fine. Natalie hoped that was true.

But a week later, the same thing happened. This time there was blood inside Willow's feed bucket—not just smatterings but what looked like gallons of it. It was disturbing to see, and Willow wasn't looking well. Natalie called the vet's office and this time demanded that Willow be seen. She wasn't going to be refused a second time.

When Natalie took Willow to the vet, the doctor scoped the offending nostril and said he couldn't find anything of concern. He mentioned that the extreme change of climate—coming into the dry, high desert air from the cooler, damp climate of Washington—might have irritated the sensitive membranes inside Willow's nostrils. He assured Natalie that horses were big animals and could afford to lose a lot of blood. He didn't seem overly concerned and sent Willow home after the examination. Natalie was relieved that it hadn't been anything worse, but she couldn't shake off the uneasiness of what she had seen. That much blood didn't seem at all normal to her. She would hate to lose Willow. The children adored her, and Natalie felt confident that she could put anyone on this horse, knowing Willow would take care of them.

Two weeks later it happened again. This time Kyla was with her mother and reached Willow first.

"Mom! Mom, come here!" was the frantic call as Kyla surveyed the scene. She had never seen so much blood, and even though her mother had told her what had been going on with Willow, seeing it in person was different. This time Willow was so weak that she could hardly load into the trailer to get to the vet's office. Kyla cried all the way there, dreading what they would be told.

"Do you think Willow will be all right?" she asked her mother through her tears. Natalie could only answer that she didn't know. They would have to wait until the vet examined her.

During Willow's first visit the vet had only scoped one of Willow's nostrils. This time, when he scoped the other, he discovered that Willow had a life-threatening disease called Guttural Pouch Mycosis, a disease that occurs when a certain fungus enters the upper respiratory tract of the horse, eventually causing severe hemorrhaging that can cause sudden death. If the diagnosis had been determined after the first nosebleed, they may have been able to save her. But now it was too late. Willow's condition had advanced beyond the point where treatment or surgery was likely to produce a good outcome. If left alone she would suffer more nosebleeds until one day she would die from loss of too much blood.

Natalie couldn't stand the thought of Willow suffering or dying alone in her pen under such traumatic circumstances. She talked to Kyla, and together they made the difficult decision to have the mare euthanized. Sweet Willow, Kyla's gentle friend, who always offered comfort and kindness to everyone and everything, was gone. Kyla was devastated.

• • •

It wasn't long after saying goodbye to Willow that another tragedy struck the Law family.

Natalie's horse Dixie, who had been doing well in endurance and was Natalie's primary riding horse, suffered a terrible accident. Dixie had been learning to pull a cart back in Washington, and Natalie liked the idea of her horses being versatile. She found that it made them better all-around athletes, and it also relieved boredom and repetition. Pulling a cart worked the horse's muscles in a different way than being ridden, while still increasing their overall fitness. Natalie had some experience with cart driving. She wasn't an expert by any means but was confident that she could continue to work Dixie with the cart and they could improve together.

The day of the accident, Natalie was working her in the large arena at the ranch, and for the first lap Dixie acted perfectly fine, floating around the arena as if there was no problem at all. However, after doing one complete lap she froze, refusing to move forward. Natalie kept pushing her forward, not wanting to end the lesson on a bad note or understanding the sudden change in the horse. In what seemed like a split-second, Dixie reared, flipped over onto her back, and ended up on the ground tangled in the harness. She struggled frantically to work herself free.

Natalie leapt from the cart and rushed toward the struggling horse. She always carried a knife, and despite the danger of the flailing hooves, she was able to get close enough to cut Dixie free of the harness and get her off the ground and away from the cart that had trapped her. It was immediately obvious that Dixie had suffered a major injury. Her heart in her throat, Natalie took Dixie straight to the vet, where X-rays revealed that she had broken several vertebrae and had shattered multiple bones in her sacrum. It was an unusual injury but not necessarily life-threatening.

Natalie blamed herself for misjudging the situation and asking so much of Dixie, especially in the midst of adjusting to a new home. She knew that Dixie was most likely overwhelmed with all the stimulus around her—the cows, the traffic, the noise she wasn't used to— and then Natalie had added more stress by asking her to do something she didn't have a lot of experience with. Sometimes, working with horses could be a humbling experience, and Natalie spent many nights crying over what she saw as her mistake. She hoped she had learned something that would prevent future accidents. Luckily, the vet felt that Dixie would have a full recovery, but she needed to be confined to a small pen that would restrict her movement and give her body time to heal. They were down to only two remaining horses of the four they had brought with them from Washington, and Natalie needed to find a different horse to ride if she wanted to continue her endurance career.

• • •

Brave and Flash had already become the best of buddies, bonding over the fact they had both been terrorized by Dixie, the lead mare. Flash didn't seem to notice that his best horse-friend towered above him in size by five hands. Standing next to each other, they resembled Arnold Schwarzenegger and Danny DeVito in the movie *Twins*. And since fate had now thrown them together as the only two horses fit to be ridden, it was lucky they got along so well. Natalie felt a few seconds of guilt for stealing her husband's horse, but she got over it quickly. The biggest problem was that Brave had hardly any trail experience and neither did Flash, let alone on the rugged and steep terrain that made up most of the trail systems around St. George.

By now, Natalie had connected with a woman named Rochelle Bromley on Facebook. Rochelle had agreed to meet Natalie and Brave at a place called Red Mountain for a trail ride. Brave had barely turned seven years old and was still learning how to control the long limbs that sprouted from his torso. On their inaugural ride with Rochelle, Brave tackled the footing like a drunken camel, his long legs flailing wildly as he tried to remain upright, his mind also flailing wildly as it tried to wrap itself around what was being asked of him. It was entertaining for Rochelle to watch, so she agreed to keep riding with Natalie for the foreseeable future.

Natalie realized right away that Brave could not handle the trails barefoot. The soles of his feet were tender. He needed not just steel shoes but pads as well to be able to tolerate his new job. Once that situation was corrected, Brave became a lot more comfortable and interested in discovering the limits that his limbs could achieve. To Rochelle's utter disappointment, the large, gangly gelding became smoother and more confident in his ability to tackle the technical and steep trails of the area. Rochelle was, of course, thrilled that Brave was improving so well, but she would miss the sheer entertainment value of seeing him tackle the trails on his first few attempts.

Rochelle introduced Natalie to a student of hers, Kacey Oar. Kacey was a teenager with a passion for horses and an interest in starting endurance riding. She needed someone to do long rides with and soon became a frequent companion to Natalie, and later Kyla, on the trails. Kacey was just a few years older than Kyla, and the two soon became good friends. It was nice for Kyla to have someone outside of her immediate family to confide in, and their friendship deepened as Kyla opened up to Kacey about her issues at school and her challenges with Flash.

Kacey's first impression of Flash was not a good one, partly because she could see how frustrating he was for Kyla to manage. To her, Flash seemed like a bundle of trouble that constantly challenged Kyla's authority and broke down her confidence. She witnessed tears of frustration as Kyla tried to work with a pony who wasn't seeming to make much headway in his training no matter how hard she tried with him. Kacey could see how much time and effort Kyla was putting into Flash and resented the pony for being so unresponsive to her efforts. She wasn't sure that Flash was deserving of the love that Kyla was pouring into him either, but it wasn't her place to say anything, so she just watched and waited to see how the situation evolved.

What Kacey was witnessing was accurate; Kyla was indeed regressing with Flash. Without Shelah's guidance, she was feeling overwhelmingly challenged by her fiery little pony. While he was somewhat rideable, his unpredictability concerned both Kyla and Natalie. Kyla was now riding Flash in the large arena at the ranch without the security of being on a lead line or being ponied by another horse. It had been six months since she and Flash had started working together. They had come a long way, but now she was having to train him on her own, without the guidance of her trusted riding instructor, who was a thousand miles away.

Just when Kyla thought Flash was settling down in the arena, he would spook and bolt, leaving Kyla to push the boundaries of her horsemanship to try and calm the pony and bring him back under control. Natalie put Kyla in a special cross-country impact vest to help cushion her falls. The vest was well tested, and Kyla could have worked as a test dummy for the company with the number of times Flash left her in a pile of dust. The unpredictability of the pony concerned even Natalie, who had a high tolerance for the risks that riding horses entailed. But Kyla pushed through the challenging times, falling often and never giving up, always getting back on and hoping she could end the session on a positive note before returning Flash to his pen.

A couple of months later, Kyla was riding Flash out on the trails without being on the lead line, and it seemed to Natalie that they were making progress. Natalie was amazed at the tenacity of her daughter. While many children may have been enthralled with the idea of befriending and teaching a cute little pony, it took determination and guts to see it through after so many frustrating setbacks and such slow progress, not to mention the frequent unplanned dismounts! Natalie saw that her daughter had grit. She pushed through things and didn't give up easily. But even Kyla, with as much love as she had developed for her best friend, had her limits.

Kyla fell into a doldrum of sorts. She became overwhelmed with the constant stress of riding Flash, never knowing what would spook him and send him bolting down the trail. She worried that she'd be hurt and began questioning her ability to train a pony like Flash, who still seemed half wild and who challenged her constantly. She loved the tiny creature with all her heart, but her self-doubt was eating away at her confidence. Was she the right person to help Flash, or had she taken on more than she could handle? Would she always be afraid, and would it ruin her love of riding forever if she couldn't find a way to make Flash more controllable and safer to ride?

The pressure built up inside her until she felt an overwhelming sense of failure. She had failed Flash, and she had failed herself by not being able to finish what she had started. She worried constantly about what would happen to him if she was unable to help him become a safe riding pony. She had heard of horses ending up in kill pens, and at night she awoke with her heart racing in her chest as she imagined Flash ending up in one of those awful places. Her sense of guilt was becoming unbearable. She cried often and felt as if the weight of the world and the fate of her pony lay upon her small shoulders.

She remembered the joy of riding a horse that she trusted and felt secure on, like her sweet Willow. She began wondering if it was all worth it. She was just a young girl, after all. Barely eleven years old. Her depression deepened. She didn't want to quit, and she didn't want to give up on the pony who meant so much to her, who she had begged her father to allow her to buy. But she couldn't get over the fact that she just didn't want to ride him anymore. Kyla was tired of feeling helpless and afraid. Finally, she asked her parents if she could have a serious talk with them.

"I know I promised that I could handle Flash when I bought him," she stammered, unable to look her parents in the eye. "But I just can't! I can't help him! I'm not a horse trainer. I'm just a kid! He needs someone older and better than me!"

She broke down in tears, devastated.

When she looked up she saw the compassion on her parents' faces. They knew she had been struggling, but they hadn't realized she had been eaten up inside with those struggles. Now they could see the extent of the pressure she had been putting on herself, and it broke their hearts.

"Flash is your pony, Kyla," Adam said softly. "It's completely up to you what you do with him." He squeezed her hand and gave her a hug, wishing that he could carry her burdens for her but knowing that was not the way the world worked. In the end, Kyla had to make her own decisions and then live with them.

Kyla put Flash up for sale, hoping that she could find a good home for him with someone who was qualified and able to continue his training. She felt a sense of relief having made the decision. Now all they had to do was wait for the right buyer to come along. Thankfully, they never did.

• • •

Natalie agreed with Adam, but the more she thought about the situation, the more the thought persisted that Kyla could be giving up too soon and may regret selling Flash. She decided to call in some back up. She flew Shelah in from Washington and reunited her with Kyla and Flash to see if she could figure out what was going on. It didn't take long for Shelah to realize that Flash had tested Kyla and had won. He hadn't done it maliciously; he just didn't know any better. He may have thought that the constant struggle to get the upper hand was a game between them, but he didn't realize that he was destroying his owner's confidence with his antics.

Shelah had a heart to heart with Kyla. Did she really want to give up on the pony she had put so much of her time and love into? If Shelah stayed with her for a few weeks and helped her, would she be prepared to give Flash another chance? With Shelah's familiar presence and no buyers for Flash looming on the horizon, Kyla agreed to get back on her still half-feral pony and give it another try.

Over the next couple of weeks, Shelah slowly helped Kyla regain her confidence. They started off small. Shelah suggested that Kyla start spending more time with Flash, simply leading him around, reestablishing the bond they had originally formed without asking too much of either of them. Kyla once more spent hours grooming him, talking with him, rebuilding the basics of their friendship that had been lost in the stress of the training program. Shelah allowed the two of them to find each other again, so when Kyla did eventually mount up to go for a ride there would be a renewed feeling of a partnership between them instead of a battle for control.

With Shelah's support they both flourished. They stayed out of the arena, which Flash honestly detested, and instead played games out on the trail, challenging Flash physically and mentally to distract him from his usual naughtiness. When Natalie joined them on the trails, Shelah noticed the way Flash and Brave interacted with each other, leaning on each other mentally as they navigated the terrain. Neither one was the leader. They were both learning, side by side, and they relied on each other to boost the other's confidence. In this way they both progressed with their training; an unlikely couple that had figured out a way to make their lives work, side by side.

Shelah and Natalie had a great idea. Kyla was in school five days a week, and Sunday mornings were dedicated to worship and service work for the Church. This didn't leave enough time for the consistent riding that Flash needed, so they devised an idea they hoped would help both Flash and Kyla whereby Natalie would start taking Flash with her whenever she was out riding Brave. At first, Natalie kept

Flash on a lead rope against Brave's side. His presence was reassuring for the larger horse, and Flash was happy to explore the trails without the stress of a rider on his back. While Brave required shoes and pads for his feet, Flash's tiny feet were rock hard and he never needed any kind of hoof protection as he happily trotted through the rocks and sandy washes without any sign of getting sore.

As some of the trails were very narrow and technical, it seemed natural for Natalie to take Flash off the lead rope so that both horses could navigate the trail more easily. Those sections became longer and longer until Natalie realized that Flash was no different than Moose, the Great Dane that often accompanied them on their rides. Moose would have his own adventures on the trail, never straying too far from Natalie and Brave, and that was exactly what Flash started to do. Sometimes Flash would run behind them; sometimes he trotted out in front. Often, he went off the trail only to come bounding back once he felt he had gone too far. Sometimes Natalie would look behind her to see Flash rolling repeatedly in the sand, first in one direction and then the other, until he would suddenly realize he had been left behind and would gallop to catch up. Natalie laughed at the little horse-dog she had created. She especially enjoyed the comments of hikers along the trail who assumed, because of his tiny size, that Flash must be Brave's foal. Natalie lost count of how many times she heard, "Oh look at the baby horse!" as they went riding by.

Flash seemed to have found a niche that suited him. Out on the trails, Flash was happier than he had ever been, and although he never seemed to get tired, it did seem to physically and mentally calm him down. On the days when Kyla rode him, he was now far more manageable. Things started to change for the better. Kyla found herself once more able to enjoy her time with him as she could now relax and enjoy riding him again. Best of all, she realized she didn't need to sell her pony after all.

CHAPTER 6

May the Duck Be with You

"There has to be a strong will to
persevere out there, mile after mile."

—BARBARA WHITE, ENDURANCE RIDER

When Shelah left to go back to Washington, she left a much happier and more confident Kyla. Kyla's excitement reignited for the next part of the journey with Flash. He was by no means perfect, but it seemed as if he was ready to give a little more effort to listening to his rider, and because he had more experience roaming free on the trails, he was also more confident when he was being ridden. Natalie decided that it was time for Brave and Flash to do an endurance ride together. It would be the first ride for them both, and Natalie decided that the Mt. Carmel XP ride, managed by Dave "The Duck" and Annie Nicholson, would be a good first ride for them both. It was a reasonable distance from St. George, so traveling to and from the ride would be easy on the horses.

Dave Nicholson, known widely as "The Duck," was quite the character. On the outside he appeared a little gruff; he didn't like to have his time wasted and had a low tolerance for riders who made his life more difficult than it already was. But if you could get the man to crack a smile, it was well worth the wait, and if you were ever in need of his extensive experience out on the trail, he was always there to help. The Duck expected riders to know how to look after their horses on the trail. His XP rides had a reputation for being remote, tough, and stunningly beautiful. His wife, Annie, worked as hard as he did. Everyone adored her, and her calm demeanor and ability to make managing a multi-day ride look easy was a testament to her expertise. Then again, she'd probably had a lot of practice managing difficult things, being married to The Duck and all.

The Nicholsons seemed to float from ride to ride throughout the year. It was hard to imagine they had a chance to lead any sort of normal life in between the rides, although their children and grandchildren proved they must have. Occasionally a Facebook post would pop up with The Duck holding a small human instead of a horse, and it was obvious which one he had more experience with. At last count they had put on no less than eleven XP rides, totaling around forty days of riding every year. That doesn't include the 2021 Lonesome Duck ride, which began at the North Rim of the Grand Canyon and crossed the state of Utah into Wyoming. That ride was by invitation only, presumably so Dave could weed out anyone he felt might be too high maintenance since the logistics of the ride were challenging enough.

The couple is well loved in the endurance world, and rightly so. Without their monumental efforts, endurance riders would have a lack of true pioneer rides to choose from, and the art of riding horses for multiple days across the wild west frontier would diminish forever. Somehow the Nicholsons have managed to get permission to hold rides in the country's most famous scenic locations—places such as Bryce Canyon, the Grand Canyon, and Death Valley. There are fewer trails than ever before to ride horses, and the Nicholsons' rides have contributed to preserving the right to cross public lands on horseback. Because of their efforts, future generations may also have the privilege of seeing our nation from the back of a horse.

Whether someone is an endurance rider or not, a foray into the XP rides website is an adventure unto itself. As well as the usual information on the rides, a plethora of examples abound of The Duck's sharp mind and dry humor. He may be a living legend who has experienced this sport as a rider, a veterinarian, and a ride manager, or he may just be a crusty old duck. Either way, a single look at the number of rides Dave and Annie manage year after year reveals that the sport of endurance would not be the same without this hard-working couple. They have been true pioneers and champions of the sport, and the sport, without a doubt, is all the better for it.

• • •

Natalie and Kyla arrived at the Mount Carmel XP ride near Kanab, Utah, in early May of 2019, ready to see how their horses would handle a fifty-mile ride and the experience of ride camp. The vetting process, where the ride vets evaluate the horse before and throughout the ride, would also be a new experience for them both. The mother and daughter team were confident they had put enough training miles on their mounts to tackle the fifty miles of trail, but there were multiple unknowns, such as how Flash would tolerate being tied to a trailer for countless hours or put into a small, portable corral.

It was a general rule that horses should be safely contained within their own area at camp. Loose horses could be a nuisance and endanger not only themselves but others as well. Another unknown was how Flash would tolerate the start of the ride, which was hard to simulate in training. There would be far more horses around than he was used to, all excited and ready to head out on the trail. Even the more experienced endurance horses could take a while to settle down on the first few miles of a ride, and for horses new to endurance the start could be especially stressful. Flash's previous fears would sometimes play out in the form of anxiety, which would then result in unpredictable behavior. Natalie desperately wanted the Mount Carmel XP ride to be a positive experience for all of them so they could continue having many more adventures at endurance rides together.

They Laws pulled into ride camp the day before they were scheduled to ride. They had only planned to ride one day, despite the multi-day venue, knowing this would be enough for their inexperienced horses. When the very tall Brave and the very short Flash approached the vetting area the next day, people exclaimed over the pair's size difference, as well as how petite Flash was. In photographs Flash had more substance to him, but in person his tiny frame and stature were far more evident. When put next to his horse-bestie, Brave, the size disparity was extraordinary.

They were an unlikely pair. It was hard to imagine that their strides could pace well together and that Flash would not expend too much energy keeping up with the larger horse. In fact, it was the exact opposite. Flash was fast, and he was unstoppable. His nifty feet carried him over the trail with a speed that belied his small frame, and it was often Brave that struggled to keep up with his tiny counterpart.

The Duck thought he had seen everything in his years of competing, vetting, and managing rides, but when presented with Flash he was somewhat speechless—although, being a man of few words, it was hard to tell.

"And what do you have here?" he asked Kyla as he began to vet Flash in.

"He's a Hackney pony," the ten-year-old replied. "This is his first endurance ride, and mine!"

The Duck raised his eyebrows but made no comment. He finished his exam, and although Flash fidgeted in protest, he didn't knock The Duck over, which was a plus.

"Well, he looks fit enough to do a ride, but are you able to ride him that far?" The Duck questioned. A flicker of a smile teased the corner of his mouth and softened his words.

"Guess I'm going to find out," Kyla blurted back, and The Duck, who appreciated personality in his horses and his riders, nodded his head in a way that, for The Duck, was actually a form of encouragement.

"I'll look forward to seeing that tomorrow," he stated and realized as he said it that he actually was.

Unfortunately, things did not go exactly as planned.

The goal was to take things slowly and try to finish within the twelve hours allotted for completion. Both Natalie and Kyla wanted to avoid rushing or pushing their horses unnecessarily. By this time, Natalie had done a few endurance rides, and Dixie had always carried her close to the front of the pack with ease. But today the strategy would be different. There were too many unknowns that both horses could experience, and Natalie was determined to ride at a conservative pace, giving Kyla and Flash the best experience they could have to officially launch their team into the sport.

They waited for most of the horses to leave camp before they mounted. Natalie knew there was a long uphill section at the beginning of the ride, and she encouraged Kyla to use that to let Flash work off a little steam, hoping he might settle down afterward. Flash looked so cute, his girl perched proudly on his back, but that first hill did nothing to slow the little hellion down. He took off down the trail as if it was his personal mission to devour every section of it as fast as possible.

"Slow down!" Kyla yelled, as she tried in vain to do just that.

But Flash flew up the uphills, cantered the downhills, trotted like a pacer at the racetrack on the flats, before unceremoniously dumping his rider at the first opportunity. Apparently he needed a little more training after all.

Once Kyla managed to remount her fire-breathing pocket dragon, the race continued in much the same way for the first twenty miles.

"Try and tuck Flash in behind Brave and don't let him go around!" Natalie called back to her daughter as Kyla continued to battle with the pony.

Natalie planted her horse directly in front of Flash to give Kyla, and theoretically Flash, a much-needed break. The thing was, Flash never really needed a break. He was happy to keep on going, and going, and going some more. Kyla had never experienced quite this type of riding and it was brutal. It became painfully clear that this was causing extreme chafing to her body, making it harder for her to control her pony. She was riding in an Australian saddle, and like all Aussie saddles there were knee rolls that her thighs could brace against on the downhills but that rubbed against her as she was posting at a rising trot. While the saddle had been fine over the shorter training distances, Kyla had now been using the knee rolls to wedge against as she pulled back on the reins, trying to slow Flash down. The knee rolls were now painfully irritating her skin.

"I can't stand it, Mom," Kyla cried. She was not a complainer, so Natalie knew it must be bad. Natalie was at a loss of how to help her daughter. They were almost halfway through the ride, and turning around to go back to camp would be nearly the same distance as continuing on the course. The only thing she could do was fall back on what she and her family always did during tough times.

"You need to pray, Kyla. God will help you through it. Just talk to Him about what's going on."

Kyla began praying her little heart out, begging for relief from the pain she was experiencing. Natalie swore to herself that from now on she would always carry something in her saddlebag in case this happened again, but for now she had nothing else to offer her daughter except the power of prayer. Apparently that was enough, as not five minutes later they rode up on a tube of Desitin laying on the trail like a gift from the heavens. Kyla could not have been happier if she had found a trough-load of goldfish snacks and candy. Her prayers had been answered in the best way possible. She dismounted and grabbed the tube as if she had just found gold. It was practically full! She spread a liberal layer of Desitin everywhere that hurt and continued the ride with extra Desitin to spare if she needed. Suddenly, life was good again.

Soon after, Natalie realized they were off course. Duck rides are marked with a mixture of ribbons and paper plates along the trail. Natalie had been distracted with Flash and Kyla's problems, and she realized in horror that she must have missed a turn. Now the four of them were out in the wilderness with no clue where they were or where they were supposed to be going. Natalie didn't remember seeing the three ribbons that would have indicated a turn, and since she didn't expect to see many ribbons on the course they could have gone miles without realizing their mistake. Her GPS was indicating that they were closing in on thirty-eight miles, and Brave was starting to show signs of tiredness.

Luckily, Flash was showing no sign of getting tired at all, and Natalie hoped that the pony would be able to encourage his friend through the rest of the ride, or at least until he found his second wind. She made the decision to double back to the last place they had seen a ribbon, looking carefully the whole way for any markings that could indicate where they may have missed a turn. After almost nine miles back in the direction they had come, they found the trail they should have taken. The horses had now done a total of forty-eight miles and still had twenty miles to go—a total of sixty-eight miles! With Flash settled down enough to take the lead, they managed to cross the finish line with just minutes to spare before the twelve-hour cutoff.

Both horses had finished their first endurance ride despite the massive side trip. Brave had indeed found a second wind toward the end and had finished well, although understandably tired by his efforts. Flash, on the other hand, was a unicorn. He was not tired at all. He arrived back at camp with a pep in his step, ready to go again. They apparently had not yet found the point where his energy became depleted. He had kept going all day, often pulling the larger Brave along, both physically and mentally. Natalie called the little renegade an emotional support pony—a name that stuck over the rides to come. He showed no signs of soreness from going barefoot and stood happily eating his hay at the trailer as if he had just completed a short ride around the neighborhood rather than sixty-eight difficult miles.

Kyla had persevered too, and Natalie could not have been prouder of the way she had worked with Flash, despite his shenanigans at the beginning. As they rolled into camp in those final minutes, The Duck looked quite relieved. He was glad he didn't have to send out a search party for the missing riders, and he had been a little worried about Kyla in particular.

"What were you doing out there?" he asked Kyla.

"Riding my pony!" she said, grinning. "I told you I could!"

Despite what they had put him through, the ride was the beginning of a friendship between The Duck, Annie, and the Laws. The Duck was impressed. Despite the rough day, neither Natalie nor Kyla complained in the slightest, which was just as well since all Duck riders who have sworn fealty to him must agree to live by The Rider Oath:

> I will not gripe, bellyache, or complain about anything pertaining to an XP ride because I realize that this is a low budget affair, and that the management does not care if I have a problem. I realize and agree that anyone who would ride an endurance ride led by a Duck has to be crazy and would not have a worthwhile opinion anyway. I am here to have a good time and if I find that I am not having a good time, I agree to pack up my things and go away, leaving the other riders and the management happy in their ignorance.

The Duck rides were challenging, fun, beautiful, and plentiful. Natalie Law knew without a doubt that she and her rather unconventional brood had found their place and their people with their new XP family.

Kyla was pleased that she and Flash had survived the ride and that he had handled the distance well. The saddle had caused some challenges, but there had also been something else bothering her when she rode—a throbbing ache in both her knees. Kyla had been an avid cross-country runner in second and third grade and had always been active. She hadn't expected her body to hurt from long distance riding, and she hoped this was a one-time thing. Maybe it flared because Flash had been misbehaving or the situation with the saddle. Whatever the cause, she hoped the next ride would be less painful.

CHAPTER 7

The Adventures of Flash, the Hackney Pony

*"Mistakes can be your strength
or your weakness, it's up to you."*

—IRIS PHILIP

In August of 2019 Natalie signed them up for two days of the Grand Canyon XP, a ride where she had placed first with Dixie the year before. The plan was to do a fifty-five-mile ride with Brave and Flash the first day. The second day Natalie would ride Dixie in the thirty-miler, while Kyla would once again ride Flash. Natalie wanted to see how her original endurance horse handled the thirty-mile ride since she'd been doing so well in her training rides at home after recovering from her injuries.

They were looking forward to visiting with the Nicholsons once again and seeing how the horses would perform this time around. Natalie and Kyla agreed that part of their strategy would be staying on the trail for this ride and not doing any "bonus" miles. Kyla was curious—would Flash tolerate two days in a row of distance riding? He might be excited to go again the next day, or he might lay down and refuse to go. He was nothing if not opinionated. Due to unforeseen circumstances, the Nicholsons had to change the venue of the ride. Instead of using the trails at the Grand Canyon, they switched the ride to the trails they managed at a Bryce Canyon ride called

The Virgin and The Outlaw. Everyone assumed that the ride name referred to Annie and The Duck.

Natalie and Kyla were still trying to figure out how to best contain Flash at ride camp. At home, he had a large pasture and had grown used to a certain level of freedom that most horses don't have. He spent much of his training time loose on the trail, going wherever he pleased. Trying to keep him tied up for several hours at a time on a high tie (a sort of bungee cord attached to an arm that stuck out at a ninety-degree angle from the trailer) or trying to contain him in a small portable corral was virtually impossible. After an accident where Flash got severe rope burn on one of his pasterns after getting hung up in the high-tie, Natalie chose to leave him loose. He was far calmer and more comfortable that way, and Natalie knew he would stay close to Brave's side. The two were inseparable as they spent more time training together. While it wasn't technically following the "rules" to have a loose horse in camp, Flash was so cute that no one complained, and he mostly stayed out of trouble.

Day one was a fifty-five-mile ride, and Kyla was looking forward to trying out her new Pandora saddle. Pandora had been following Flash and Kyla's adventures, and after seeing them finish the ride at Mount Carmel they decided to do a partial sponsorship for Kyla with one of their lightweight endurance saddles. The Pandora saddle weighed only three pounds compared to the Australian saddles' twenty-five. It was far easier for Kyla to handle as she tacked and untacked her pony, and it reduced the amount of weight that Flash had to carry. The reduction in saddle weight also offset the weight increase from Kyla's growing body. Flash looked very dapper, decked out in his flashy new endurance gear!

Natalie and Kyla waited for most of the other horses to leave camp that morning before heading out. It was Brave and Flash's second ride together, and Natalie wanted things to be as calm and stress free as possible from the start. They headed out of camp and down the trail. A nice lady raised her hand in greeting as they rode past, commenting on how cute Flash looked. Flash was used to his adoring fans by now and seemed to know when to add a little extra pep to his step.

All experienced endurance riders will tell you to *never* experiment with new tack and accessories at a ride. You never know if things are going to rub at mile forty-eight that seemed fine at mile five. It's just good policy to use equipment that is well proven, just in case. But since Kyla loved snacking on goldfish crackers and candy, Natalie had decided to add a pair of saddlebags to Flash's tack for all of Kyla's stuff. It had seemed like a great idea.

A quarter mile out of camp, as Flash picked up the trot, all hell broke loose.

"Mom! *Mooomm!*" Kyla screamed as Flash bolted forward, saddlebags flapping against his sides.

"Do a one-rein stop," Natalie yelled as she realized what was happening.

Kyla tried turning him in circles to slow him down but eventually gave up and bailed into a bush that offered a softer landing than the ground. As she lay in the bushes, Kyla had flashbacks to the previous ride where Flash had also dumped her close to the start. There seemed to be an emerging pattern. Flash, now free of his rider, bid the group farewell and galloped the quarter mile back to camp, almost knocking over the nice lady who had thought he was so cute a few minutes earlier. He probably appeared less cute barreling toward her riderless and out of control.

Kyla got up. Trooper that she was, she hiked back to camp behind her mom and Brave. She removed the offending saddlebags and gamely climbed back into the saddle to try again.

The trails on this ride were indeed spectacular, but they were also the most technical trails that Natalie and Kyla had done so far. Flash was still barefoot, partly because he had never shown any sign of soreness in his travels so far, and partly because his hooves were so tiny that Natalie and Kyla hadn't really figured out what they could put on them anyway. The ride tested them all, mentally and physically, with steep climbs, drop offs, and narrow trails that led through loose patches of shale with barely any decent footing to rely on. Flash got so tired of the footing that he chose to move off the trail and ride to the side of it, jumping over any obstacles in his way.

They reached the vet check and recovered the crew bags they had sent to the lunch stop. Despite some nervous moments, Kyla was having a great time. Annie had made her famous sandwiches for the riders. She spoiled them with large piles of turkey, ham, or egg salad sandwiches that filled the riders' hungry stomachs. The rest of the ride was equally spectacular, and both horses completed sound and happy and with great vet scores.

Natalie noted that while Flash pulsed down as soon as he entered the vet checks, Brave would come off the trail with a heart rate of about eighty beats per minute. It took a few minutes for him to reach the ride criteria of sixty beats per minute. As he got further along in his career, his recoveries improved, but for now it was something that Natalie had to work with.

On day two, Kyla rode Flash in the thirty-mile ride, and Natalie switched to Dixie, the Saddlebred that had been her original endurance horse and who had shown so much promise until the terrible cart accident. Nine months and a strong recovery later, Natalie was hopeful she could return to competing in endurance rides with Dixie. Dixie flew along the thirty-mile course, easily maintaining a twelve-mile-an-hour trot on any good sections of trail with Flash happily keeping pace.

Flash had been eager to get back on the trail, and Kyla was excited to see how he would do on their second day. She still hadn't pushed him to the point of tiredness, and toward the end of the ride Flash flew past Dixie for a second-place finish. Kyla was thrilled with her little pony's performance. He had triumphed on a tough course, covering eighty-five miles in the two days they competed. This made Kyla and Natalie wonder if the Hackney breed overall had the natural athleticism needed for endurance, or if Flash was an exception. They weren't aware of any other Hackneys competing, but for Flash, at least, the breed seemed a natural fit for the sport.

Dixie had done well, but a couple of miles from the finish Natalie realized her horse was showing some intermittent mild soreness on her front right foot. When she trotted out for the vet, she was slightly lame and didn't receive a completion. Natalie was disappointed, but Dixie had done well overall and had demonstrated she had recovered from the accident.

Brave had been a total rock star the day of his ride, and Natalie had been thrilled with his performance. He had transformed into a stunning gelding with the sleek coat and mature musculature of an endurance athlete. The ride weekend was a success. Both Brave and

Flash were capable of doing the miles and the pace to complete endurance rides, and most importantly, seemed to be having fun doing them. Fortunately, Dixie just had a stone bruise from stepping on a rock on the trail and recovered quickly.

But one dark cloud hovered over the weekend—Kyla's knees had once again hurt throughout the ride. She had taken some Tylenol at the beginning of the second day, and Natalie had rubbed a little Surpass ointment onto them—a topical anti-inflammatory cream for horses, but it wouldn't be the first time a rider used the horses' medicine stash for their own uses!

"We're going to have to make you a doctor's appointment to see why your knees are hurting you so much," Natalie remarked. She could easily see how much discomfort Kyla was in by the end of the ride.

"But what if it's something really bad?" Kyla nervously bit her lower lip.

"It's better that we know what you're dealing with now so we can fix it," Natalie responded, wondering what could be causing such pain at that young age. Flash's tiny stature meant he took far more steps throughout the course of the ride, so Kyla had to rise out of the saddle and post more frequently than if she had been on a larger horse. Natalie wondered if simply the fact that her daughter had to work so much harder than most over long distances was causing the problem.

• • •

Kyla was still being bullied in school and picked on by her peers. Things had improved slightly since moving to Utah, but she still saw herself as an outsider. She realized that her mother was right—there would be people throughout her life who didn't like her and she would have to learn to deal with it. It was easier said than done. There were many days where she would rush down to the barn after school, give Flash his mash, clamber onto his back, and lay down on him as she told him about her day. He had become used to this routine and was a wonderful listener. Even once he had finished his mash he would stand there, occasionally shifting his weight from side to side, but remaining still as he listened to Kyla's troubles.

"I don't understand it, Flash!" Kyla would tell him tearfully. "I didn't do anything to them, and they are just so mean and horrible to me! Thank goodness I have you to talk to. What would I do without you in my life?"

Flash's acceptance of her, as well as his warm coat and steady breathing, comforted her like nothing else could. But the fact that Kyla could so easily climb onto him bareback presented a looming problem. She was growing taller, and her long legs were beginning to hang below Flash's belly. Although Flash didn't seem bothered at all, Kyla knew she was on borrowed time with her pony, and it was extremely upsetting. Kyla had put so much time into getting Flash ready to be ridden. It had taken years to build the solid bond of trust they now shared, and she couldn't imagine a world where she would no longer be able to ride him. What would happen to him then? She felt a constant pressure in their race against time to accomplish a few more rides together before she outgrew her pony. Everyone but Flash, who was blissfully unaware, knew the clock was ticking.

Kyla had no idea that everything she had been through with Flash was developing her character and turning her into a young woman worthy of recognition for her efforts. While other kids were watching TV or sitting in their rooms obsessed with their phones, Kyla was riding Flash across the broad landscape of the Wild West. She was also enjoying the time she was spending with her mother. Not many kids got to spend hours with a parent doing what they both loved, and although sometimes they rode quietly, enjoying the beautiful scenery around them, they also spent a lot of time talking about life, faith, and all those things they might never have had time to discuss if riding didn't offer them that opportunity.

Natalie was also enjoying the closeness that endurance riding was bringing to her and Kyla's relationship, while at the same time battling the guilt that she had three other children who needed her time and attention as well. When she wasn't riding, she was working at home helping Adam with his business and chauffeuring their children to school, after-school events, and all the activities that revolved around their church and community. Although a frantic life at times, Natalie was determined to continue doing what she loved with her horses and keep her family and husband happy at the same time. As soon as they were back home from the ride at Bryce Canyon, she signed herself and Kyla up for a fifty-mile ride in Scottsdale, Arizona, that December.

Natalie also came to a decision about Dixie. The horse had healed quickly and had shown that she was ready to return to endurance, but Natalie had become extremely attached to Brave, as had Flash. Because Dixie had such a huge trot, Brave was a much better match for Flash out on the trails.

Natalie knew she didn't have time to compete on two horses and all the training that entailed, so she arranged with Shelah Wetter to trade Dixie for a three-year-old Saddlebred named Coco that she could begin slowly training while riding Brave as her main endurance horse.

Natalie decided to find an endurance ride where Shelah could easily meet them to do the trade, and where Shelah could see how Flash and Kyla were doing together and crew for them. She chose the fifty-mile Mary and Anne Memorial Ride. That October, they were packed and headed to La Pine, Oregon.

• • •

The ride in Oregon was a truly miserable experience for many reasons. Before leaving Utah, Kyla had rescued two baby mice whose mother had abandoned them in their nest, and she had brought them along to the ride so she could take care of them. She kept them snuggled inside her jacket pocket, but at the beginning of the ride meeting on Friday, she discovered they had both died. She was inconsolable and cried throughout the whole meeting.

"I killed them, Mom! I'm a murderer!"

"What did you use to feed your snake, Kyla?" Natalie asked, after trying to console her daughter and failing.

"Mice! But that was different! I was trying to *save* these ones!" Kyla bawled.

Life, Natalie realized next to a grief-stricken Kyla, was all about perspective.

Misery number two happened much later that evening. Natalie became violently ill and spent two terrible, middle-of-the-night hours in a freezing porta potty with a wrenching stomachache, throwing up into the urinal. She lost track of how many times she asked herself why she was still even contemplating doing the ride in the morning, but somehow found herself mounted on Brave at the starting line. She was a born endurance rider, able to overcome difficulty and discomfort and ride regardless.

Then, to add insult to injury, the weather took a drastic turn for the worse. They had known it wasn't going to be great; the forecast predicted wind, snow, hail, and more wind for the day of the ride, but it was worse than they had imagined. Even though the horses had their winter coats they were miserable throughout the ride, probably wondering why their humans thought a ride in this weather was necessary. Natalie and Kyla had managed to secure another sponsor and were kitted out in the best winter riding gear by Kerrits. It helped keep them as warm and dry as possible, but even so, it was miserable being out all day in those conditions.

The horses performed well despite the weather, and amazingly Kyla found herself racing in against Barbara Ott, a long-time endurance rider and recent Tevis finisher, for a second place finish. She confessed later that she had encouraged Flash to speed up at the end, even while yelling, "Sorry! Wild pony!" as she darted around Barbara just before the finish. It appeared that the bad weather had brought out the competitive side of Kyla's nature!

Even though both horses finished strong they had a difficult time after the ride. The weather had taken its toll on all of them. Flash, as small as he was, was struggling with the freezing temperatures and the biting wind. Kyla put four blankets on him, and still he shivered beneath them. Brave was doing better but having a miserable time of it still, so they rallied around the horses, feeding them warm mash to thaw them out and encourage good gut sounds. Natalie worried that she had not given the horses enough electrolytes during the ride and was concerned there was something other than the weather causing the horses' distress, something they could have prevented.

Natalie realized that she and Kyla still had a lot to learn about endurance and would be constantly challenged and tested as they rode their horses through different temperature extremes and terrain over the next few years. She had lengthy discussions with Max and Darlene Merlich about what they could have done differently, what changes they could implement to their feed, and how they could improve their electrolyte program to better help their horses. Natalie was not afraid to ask for help and was constantly building relationships with those who had more experience in the sport. As she quickly found, endurance is full of people more than happy to act as mentors, and Max and Darlene were two of the best.

As people started paying more attention to Flash, Natalie decided that it would be fun to give Flash his own Facebook page, and she launched The Adventures of Flash, the Hackney Pony soon after. Natalie chronicled his endurance rides and training progress, showed his followers how he ran loose on training rides next to his friend Brave, and posted photographs of Flash and Kyla together, just enjoying life. Natalie had a feeling that the pony would be of interest to endurance riders and to members of The American Hackney Horse Society, who would be thrilled to see how Flash was representing the breed. The sport of endurance was changing as other breeds of horses stepped up to the challenge. It was becoming more common to see mustangs and a plethora of gaited breeds hitting the trail, and Natalie was pleased that she and Kyla were demonstrating how very different horse breeds could do well, even against their Arabian counterparts who had traditionally dominated the sport.

When they returned to Utah, Natalie took Kyla to her appointment with an orthopedic doctor. He examined her and told Natalie that he was fairly sure the pain was caused by the speed of Kyla's growth spurt. It was a common issue in teenagers, especially teenage athletes. However, he scheduled X-rays and an MRI of her knees to make sure there were no structural issues causing the pain. After the tests they met with the doctor to discuss the results. The good news was that there was nothing structurally wrong. The bad news was that Kyla *was* growing fast and there was very little they could do about it other than Tylenol, ice, massages, and a topical painkiller.

As Kyla was getting taller, her bones were growing faster than her connective tissue could keep up with, putting stress on her joints. Asking her body to work hard on long distance rides added to the aggravation her knees were already experiencing, and only she could make the decision of whether she would continue riding through the pain. Kyla was glad there was nothing more serious wrong with her, but she was also extremely frustrated that the pain was becoming harder to manage. She had years of growing ahead. Did that mean that she would be in pain throughout her whole teenage years? The doctor didn't have a definitive answer. They would just have to wait and see.

• • •

They finished the 2019 ride season with the fifty-mile ride in Scottsdale, Arizona. This ride was sanctioned by the Equine Distance Riding Association, EDRA, the same organization that had run the Oregon ride in October. Dennis and Suzanne Sommers, who Natalie also considered mentors for her and Kyla, ran the organization.

The scenery in Arizona was beautiful. Hundreds of magnificent saguaro cactus crawled up the hillsides around them, standing guard over the trails they would be passing along the next day. The weather for this ride would be crisp and beautiful—typical winter desert weather and thankfully very different from their previous ride in Oregon. The ride went well, although at one point Flash bolted and Kyla found herself bailing onto a cactus. The prickly landing encouraged her to stay on for the rest of the ride since there were no good places to land on these desert trails. Kyla was worried that Flash would end up in a cactus himself or get the dreaded cholla cactus stuck in his tail or attached to his legs and body. The cholla seemed to jump onto anything that went by and were awful to remove. They weren't fun for the rider that had a run-in with them either!

Brave and Flash were continuing to place well together, and despite Flash's occasional unruly behavior, it was clear that he and Kyla were, at least, making progress. In fact, Flash pulled off a second place finish, making it clear to everyone who saw him that the little Hackney pony and the young girl riding him were a formidable team. Flash was performing as well as horses much larger than he was, and Natalie began to think about whether they might enter the Tevis Cup—the granddaddy of all modern endurance rides—in July of 2020. It was a lofty goal this early in their career, but it was obvious that Kyla and Flash had limited time left to compete together. Maybe Tevis was something they needed to seriously consider.

After the ride they sat down with various friends and mentors—the Sommers, Kathleen Pilo, Sandra and Guy Cheek, and Darlene and Max Merlich. Natalie was excited with how well the horses had done and wanted to pick the brains of these people she respected and who had experienced the Tevis Cup ride themselves. She was sure Tevis should be their next goal to shoot for in endurance. The horses were flying down the trail, and she and Kyla were enjoying going to the rides together and meeting all the wonderful new people who were coming into their lives because of the sport. It wasn't just Flash who was doing well. Brave was proving to be a wonderful endurance partner and formidable competitor too, and Natalie was proud of how well her handsome Brave was doing.

When Natalie brought up the idea to the group, she sensed their hesitation. All admitted that Brave and Flash had the talent to set a goal for Tevis at some point in the future, but they were concerned about the horses' ability to take on a ride as tough as Tevis so early in their careers. Natalie respected the opinions of these more experienced riders and realized that she and Kyla still had a lot to figure out about riding their horses over longer distances, and maybe it *was* too early to be thinking about Tevis. But the Tevis seed was planted, and on their way home to Utah, the two of them discussed their growing dreams of challenging themselves and their horses over tougher courses with the ultimate goal of entering the Tevis Cup.

Despite the advice from their mentors, Natalie couldn't shake the fact that doing the Tevis Cup in 2020 may be the only chance Kyla would have of attempting the iconic ride on Flash. It might be worth pushing themselves a little harder so that she and Kyla could have that experience together. The more she thought about it, the more she realized they may need to give it a try. She felt confident in their horses' abilities and after the success of the horses at the Scottsdale ride, she felt that nothing could stop them.

Nothing, of course, except a worldwide pandemic.

CHAPTER 8

The Imperfect Storm

"Create experiences that leave you in awe,
for those will be the highlights of your life."

—RYAN BLAIR

The Tevis Cup started the modern format of endurance riding in North America today. It inspired and influenced the sport around the world and is on the bucket list of many serious endurance competitors The Tevis Cup website provides information to help the horse, rider, and crew plan and prepare for the ride. The rider must meet a minimum criterion to enter with a total of 300 sanctioned miles of rides, and the equine must be at least six years old by the date of the ride to compete. There is now a limit of 210 participants, and the ride fills up quickly, although that changes as the event gets closer and entrants cancel for a variety of reasons. Many things can go wrong leading up to the ride and everything gets blamed on the unlucky little creatures known as the Tevis gremlins. If something prevents you from starting or finishing the Tevis Cup, it was the Tevis gremlins that got you! The ride itself has a daunting completion rate of only 49 percent. Many have tried to complete the Tevis Cup several times and failed before finally crossing the finish line another year to win the coveted silver belt buckle, a reward that makes them a member of one of the most exclusive clubs on earth.

The ride has a certain aura surrounding it, an aura that invites people from all walks of life to come together and take on the monumental challenge along a trail that runs from Robie Park, near Lake Tahoe, to the historic gold rush town of Auburn, California. It may be the historic trail itself that inspires awe, or the characters that make up its history, but there is a sense of reverence when people speak of the Tevis Cup. To be enfolded in its magic is something that most big dreamers in the sport of endurance aspire to, and even those who volunteer or crew for the event can feel the enormity of the challenge and appreciate the history of a ride where decades of teams have suffered, survived, and become one with the dust and dirt of this trail.

The Tevis Cup attracts riders from all over the world. A banquet is held in their honor—the foreign rider's banquet—to recognize their efforts and welcome them as they take on the challenge of a lifetime. They must ride borrowed or leased horses, stay with a host family, and deal with the added challenge of jet lag in addition to the usual nerves and excitement of the race. Undoubtedly, whether they finish or not, they fly home with a lifetime of memories and stories to tell that will make every moment worth it.

The Tevis Cup is more than just a ride or a race—it's a continuation of history, a trail that can crush dreams or make them come true. It represents the spirit of the Wild West and the tough and hardy souls that have crossed its mountains. It has beauty and brawn. There is glory in the sheer magnificence of the challenge.

In 2020, COVID-19 struck the nation and changed everything. With the world in uproar, no one knew how their daily lives would be affected or if things would ever return to normal. There were toilet paper shortages, and bleach was being ripped from the shelves as if it were holy water. For the first few months of the year endurance rides halted across the country as everyone grappled with the safest way to continue holding events.

Due to the enormity of organizing the Tevis Cup, and the fact that teams came from all over the world, the Tevis organizers made the difficult but necessary decision to cancel the ride. Tevis had only been canceled once since its inception in 1955 due to wildfires on the trail in 2008. With Tevis canceled, Natalie and Kyla both knew that Kyla had missed her chance to ever ride Flash in the iconic race. There was no way she would fit him in eighteen months, when hopefully the world would be normal once again and the 2021 Tevis Cup ride would take place.

Gradually, rides in certain parts of the country began to return. The Nicholsons started the XP rides back up once they had safety measures in place, and others followed. Certain states were less restricted than others, and these states allowed endurance rides to take place, often limiting the number of riders who could attend. Crews were discouraged—the fewer people around the better—and masks were required at camp and at the vet checks, but the rides slowly began to return.

In May of 2020 Kyla and Flash completed fifty-five miles at Mount Carmel, one of their favorite rides. Other than the fact that Kyla was devastated that Annie would not be making her famous sandwiches for the lunch vet check, the ride was much the same as any other year. Kyla placed second, beginning an avalanche of top placings for her and Flash that year. They placed first over three days of rides at The Virgin and The Outlaw, and they decided that their year of successful rides would culminate in their first ever one-hundred-mile ride.

Natalie and Kyla each had different reasons for attempting the hundred. For Natalie it was to challenge Brave and see if he could, indeed, ever be a Tevis horse. He had surprised her with his willingness to move down the trail ride after ride. He was becoming more efficient with his gaits and more savvy in his knowledge of pacing on the trail. His heart rate recoveries were improving, which demonstrated that his overall fitness was improving also. It was time to put him to the test on a longer course.

Kyla was painfully aware that her time with Flash was ending— she was simply getting too tall to ride him any longer. This, as well as the situation with her knees, forced her to accept that they only had until the end of the year to work together. It seemed a cruel irony that just as they were beginning to truly make progress with their partnership, time was stripping them of any further opportunities. Kyla wanted to do something spectacular to end their career together. They had done numerous fifty-mile rides and many multi-day rides by this time, so their final event together would *have* to be a one-hundred-mile ride. This would be the culmination of three years of effort to become the team they were today, and she wanted them to go out on top, with a glorious finish to their career and their unique partnership.

The Remarkable Scottsdale 100 was held in December, and Natalie signed them up for their first—and for Kyla and Flash, their last—one-hundred-mile ride. Kyla looked forward to the ride, but her anticipation was tinged with sadness at the finality of it. She knew she would go on to do other rides on different horses, but her focus had been on Flash for so long that she couldn't imagine having a relationship with another horse like she had with him. Her friend, Kacey Oar, also signed up for the ride, and they planned on traveling from Utah together. Having Kacey around would alleviate the sadness Kyla knew she would experience, and since Kacey would be doing the fifty-mile ride on her horse, she would finish in time to help crew for Natalie and Kyla on the last part of their ride.

Ten days before they were due to leave for Arizona Kyla got the worst ear infection of her life. It was debilitating, and she was unable to ride Flash or help her mother pack for the upcoming trip. She started on a series of antibiotics and hoped she would be well enough to attend the event. The antibiotics did their job and, although not completely recovered, Kyla felt she was well enough to join her mother and Kacey.

On the drive, Kyla and Kacey couldn't help but talk about Kyla's final ride on Flash.

"Have you really wrapped your head around it, Kyla, that this will be your last endurance ride on him?" Kacey asked.

"I'm not sure," Kyla started. "Sometimes I forget because he still feels the same to me."

"Maybe you can find another horse to ride next year," Kacey suggested hopefully. "Christmas is coming up!"

"Don't go getting any ideas," Natalie called back from the front seat. "Let's just get this ride done first, and then we can talk about next year after that."

"It doesn't matter, anyway," Kyla said sadly. "I won't ever love another horse like I love Flash. He means everything to me."

They drove in silence for a while, each one absorbing the finality of what Kyla and Flash were about to do.

• • •

By the time they arrived and settled the horses in at ride camp, Natalie had begun feeling under the weather. She didn't have any particular symptoms she could pinpoint, but her energy was low and she barely had an appetite. She wondered if she was feeling the pressure of riding a one-hundred-mile race more than she realized. Although Shelah had promised to come and crew for them, it was too risky to travel all the way from Washington state with the unknowns of Covid. As Kyla's ear infection continued to improve, Natalie continued to get worse. By the morning of the ride, it was all she could do to head out on what she knew would be the most difficult challenge of her endurance career so far. But she was there, and nothing was going to stop her. She wanted to test Brave in his first hundred, but more than that she wanted her daughter to have the best experience she could on her final career ride on Flash.

The scenery in Scottsdale was just as beautiful as it had been the year before. Tall saguaros stretched toward the sky, and the desert gifted them with perfect temperatures and clear skies. Although the evenings were chilly, the daytime temperatures were perfect for winter endurance rides. The footing for the horses was good, with the hardest part of the ride being the overall distance. For Natalie, especially, the ride never seemed to end. They rode part of the ride with Dennis Sommers, who at one time had expressed his doubts that Flash could ever be an endurance mount. He was eating his words. Dennis was amazed at how Flash ate up the trails and at how well he and Kyla worked as a team. Kacey had also noticed the change in Flash. He was now taking his role as Kyla's partner seriously, hardly pulling any shenanigans and moving down the trail as if he were on a mission.

About halfway through the ride, Brave started to seem a little off. It was subtle, a slight change in his gait here and there, but Natalie was thankful there was a vet check just ahead where he could be evaluated. Natalie became more stressed as she rode the last couple of miles into the vet check. If Brave was pulled for lameness, it would be the end of not only her ride but Kyla's also. There was no one else who could sponsor a junior through the rest of the ride, as they were the only two entered in that distance. The good news was that if they completed sound, they would be guaranteed a first and second place.

It ended up being no more than a loose shoe, and Natalie breathed a sigh of relief. Once it was fixed, Brave trotted out beautifully and there were no further issues—other than the fact that Natalie was exhausted and needed to take a long nap before she could complete the final loop of the ride. Since both horses had kept up a good pace throughout the day, they were still well within their twenty-four-hour time limit to finish. A little rest would do them all good. Natalie was proud of how well Brave was doing, even seventy-five miles into the ride. She had quite the horse. He was strong, powerful, and willing, and he also had a kind and giving nature. She was glad she had stolen him from Adam!

Kyla was enjoying the ride, but as night closed in and they found themselves riding alone in the desert, anxiety started crowding her chest. She still wasn't feeling 100 percent—maybe that was contributing to her fast-beating heart—but this was her first time riding in the dark, and she didn't like it. The saguaros and ocotillos created strange moonlit shadows on the trail, and she could hear the coyotes in the desert, their soulful howls echoing all around her.

"Mom, that coyote sounded close," she told Natalie nervously.

"It's fine, Kyla. A coyote isn't going to bother a horse."

"Maybe not your horse, but what about mine? He's tiny!"

Flash was so small—he must look like something a pack of coyotes could easily take down. Kyla's imagination was getting the better of her, and in that moment she was glad this would be her last ride.

They finished the one hundred miles, each grateful in their own way that the ride was over. Kyla's knees were inflamed with pain, and riding in the darkness had taken its toll. Natalie was feeling worse than before and decided she would never do another one-hundred-mile ride again.

"I'd have to be crazy to put myself through that again!" she told Kacey as she handed Brave to her and collapsed into bed.

Kyla untacked Flash and made sure he was fed and watered before going to bed herself. Even though she was exhausted, she couldn't fall asleep. She lay awake, her journey that day with Flash repeating in her mind. More than that, the whole of their journey circled her thoughts.

She remembered how terrified he had been of everything when they first met. She remembered giving up, putting him up for sale, and then how, with Shelah's help, they had found each other again, connecting in a way that made their bond even stronger.

Flash had carried her one hundred miles that day. It was a huge feat for any horse, but especially for one Flash's size. He had never faltered. Both horses had carried their riders to a successful finish at a tough ride and had now joined the elite club of one-hundred-mile endurance horses. It was a magnificent end to a year held hostage by a pandemic. Kyla and Flash had risen to a challenge beyond any they could ever have imagined.

CHAPTER 9

Never Say Never

"What you are is God's gift to you,
what you become is your gift to God."

—HANS URS VON BALTHASAR

Natalie sat down with Kyla and her younger sister Layla and laid things out for them. Kyla could still ride Flash occasionally, but he would need a new pilot if he were going to continue doing endurance rides. Would Layla be up for the challenge? The other big question, of course, was whether Flash would accept Layla as a rider.

Layla had only ridden Flash once before at a thirty-mile ride the previous October. The whole ride had been a bit of a disaster and was much harder than they anticipated, taking over seven hours to finish the thirty miles. Natalie wasn't sure if Layla would be on board to ever ride Flash again after that experience.

Flash was most definitely Kyla's horse. In his mind, Kyla was his girl. He didn't seem particularly interested in having anyone other than Kyla on his back. He had not been happy when Layla had rudely been stuck up there. The energy of the two girls could not have been more different. Kyla was calm and steady; Layla was young and expressive—something Flash had a real problem with at the beginning of his training. However, Layla was motivated to complete a fifty-mile ride while she was still *eight* years old, simply because Kyla had been *nine* years old when she did her first fifty-mile ride! She saw it as a challenge.

Even though Flash was really only trained for Kyla to ride, Natalie felt that if Layla was up for the task, Flash would eventually adjust to having a new rider. She hoped that Kyla would help her sister by teaching her how to handle him so they could bond as a team. Kyla begrudgingly handed over the reins to Layla and watched with interest to see what would happen.

Layla had been around horses all her life, even back when the family had lived in Washington. She had been included in the riding lessons at Shelah Wetter's, but she had been so young back then that she had just learned the basics: how to sit, hold the reins, and balance as the horse walked around the arena.

Layla was the baby of the family, with long, blonde, curly hair, blue eyes, and cute dimples. She was precocious and adorable. She and Flash were visually a great match and, in truth, they had similar personalities. But that was not necessarily a good thing. With Layla willing to give endurance riding a chance, Natalie began to fill in the next few ride entries with Layla as Flash's new rider.

With the goodwill of Christmas permeating the Law household, Kyla wrote up a sales agreement saying that Flash could temporarily belong to Layla over the next few years until she also outgrew him; then he would revert to Kyla's ownership.

"It's not forever, Layla," she reminded her sister. "Once you stop riding him, his ownership reverts right back to me. But in the meantime, I guess you can take him over. Merry Christmas."

These last two words were spoken without much Christmas cheer. Kyla knew that it was inevitable that Layla would be taking him over and felt that if Layla saw Flash as her own horse, she would work harder to create a bond with him and become a team. It was a kind gesture and well intentioned, although Kyla could not shake the heartbreak she felt at no longer being Flash's only person. Natalie could see the pain it was causing Kyla but encouraged her daughter to be pragmatic and accept that change was inevitable.

• • •

Natalie knew she may well have had the coronavirus at the time of the Scottsdale ride in December since her mother came down with the same symptoms and tested positive soon after they had returned. This would explain why she had felt so much worse on the one-hundred-mile ride than she expected, and why she had been so exhausted.

But with the pain of the ride a distant memory, by a couple of weeks anyway, the thought of entering Tevis really took hold. If she could get through a one-hundred-mile ride with the virus, how much easier would it be if she were healthy? Natalie knew she had an excellent horse in Brave, and after seeing how he had tackled the Scottsdale ride, she felt confident he'd be ready for Tevis in July. With much excitement, she filled in her Tevis entry form and sent it to the Tevis Cup organizers, hoping the ride would not be derailed once again by the continuing pandemic.

Natalie wondered how Brave would manage without Flash, his emotional support pony. Brave leaned on Flash to pull him through the tougher parts of the rides. He fed off Flash's energy, and even though his name was Brave, sometimes he wasn't. Natalie was also disappointed that the dream of her and Kyla doing the Tevis Cup together was not going to happen. Layla would be far too inexperienced to attempt such a challenge, and Natalie now faced the reality that she would be doing Tevis alone. She thought about asking Shelah to ride with her but knew that Tevis had never been on Shelah's bucket list. Besides, she would need Shelah on the ground crewing for her.

Then, on January 11, 2021, the Tevis organization announced that first-time junior riders, or junior riders that had not completed the Tevis Cup ride before, could ride free that year. While cost was not the determining factor, the emphasis on junior riders entering the ride got Natalie's mind churning again. If there was even a slight chance that she and Kyla could ride together at Tevis after all, shouldn't they go for it? Maybe Kyla wouldn't grow much more between now and then. Besides, even though she was getting taller, Kyla still only weighed eighty-seven pounds. If her growth slowed down, maybe the pain in her knees would lessen and she would feel up to the challenge of doing another one-hundred-mile ride, especially to fulfill one of the goals they had discussed pursuing before Covid changed everything. Most of all, Natalie realized that she wasn't quite ready to give up on the idea of doing the biggest adventure of them all with Kyla.

Even though the Remarkable Scottsdale 100 had been a remarkable end to Kyla's career with Flash, it would also be an even more dramatic end to Kyla and Flash's story for them to do the Tevis Cup together. Kyla would be turning thirteen in April, just three months before the ride. Would it be fair to ask Flash to do a ride that long, and that tough, with a growing teenager on his back? Natalie tortured herself with these questions for days, never mentioning her thoughts to Kyla. Then she realized who would be the perfect person to help her decide if this was something she should even be considering.

Natalie put in a call to Shelah Wetter. Shelah was one of the few people who knew Flash, Kyla, and the world of endurance well enough to help Natalie make an informed decision. Their conversation went something like this.

NATALIE: So, Tevis is offering junior riders a free entry this year. It got me thinking, could Flash still carry Kyla through Tevis in July if she doesn't grow much more by then?

SHELAH: Absolutely. He's tough!

Well, that was easy!

Then Natalie went to Kyla.

NATALIE: So, Shelah thinks you could do Tevis with Flash this year, so long as you don't grow too much more. Would you still like to try and ride Flash at the Tevis Cup if it were possible?

KYLA: Yes! Yes, absolutely! Let's go for it!

And the decision was made.

Kyla couldn't believe it! Even after sending in her application, she knew that participating in Tevis wasn't assured, but it drew her out of the sadness she had been experiencing, thinking her time with Flash was over. It gave her a thread of hope to hang on to and a dream to pursue.

• • •

It was late January of 2021. They had just a few short months to tweak their training and plan their rides leading up to Tevis. When Natalie filled out the Tevis entry form she realized there was something a little different about her application. In filling out the information about the horses, Natalie had already signed up a 16'3" hand Saddlebred and was now entering an 11'2" hand Hackney pony. She realized they would be riding the tallest and the smallest horses at Tevis that year. In fact, Flash would be the smallest horse to ever complete the iconic ride if he finished. He and Kyla had the chance to make Tevis history. No pressure there.

They decided as a family that Layla should still compete on Flash leading up to Tevis, with Kyla doing a multi-day ride on him a month or two before, just to make sure the saddle and stirrup length would still work for her and that Flash could still carry her comfortably. Natalie would continue to take Flash on training rides with Brave and let him run loose, thereby keeping his fitness levels up without the weight of a rider on his back. Kyla would need to do some rides on other horses so she would be in shape for the one hundred miles at Tevis, and they would experiment with different ways to help her knees, like using a knee brace during longer rides. They had a plan in place. So long as Flash and Layla got along, everything would go smoothly.

Unfortunately, all of Kyla's efforts to teach Layla about Flash had fallen on deaf ears, resulting in a battle of wills between a headstrong eight-year-old girl and an eleven-year-old tyrannical pony. Most of the conversations between the sisters regarding Flash didn't go well:

"Layla, you have to turn him if he tries to run off with you. Don't just scream! It makes him worse."

"I hate it when he runs off! It's terrifying!"

"Then practice turning him! You have to be the boss or he won't respect you."

"I don't think he likes me!"

"Well, you're probably right! But you still have to learn how to control him!"

Layla looked up to her big sister in all things, but for some reason she just wasn't paying attention to Kyla's efforts to help her with Flash. After further failed attempts by Kyla to help her sister, Natalie decided to enter Layla and Flash in a fifty-mile endurance ride. By the end of the ride, they should have sorted out their issues. Or not.

Natalie signed them up for the Antelope Island ride in April. Antelope Island is the largest island in the Great Salt Lake in Utah. It covers an area over twenty-eight thousand acres and is home to bison, antelope, pronghorn, and mule deer, as well as numerous waterfowl. The island also has the prestigious history of having had the largest sheep shearing operation west of the Mississippi in the 1930s and is another of those bucket list rides that endurance riders pursue.

For the fifty-mile ride on day one, Natalie once again had a gaggle of juniors with her. Kyla was riding a young Saddlebred they called Flair, Kacey was coming along with one of her own horses, and Layla would be on Flash. On the second day, most of the kids would go to a nearby amusement park with Adam. Natalie planned on riding Brave the first day on the fifty and then riding Coco, her young and upcoming Saddlebred, the next day on the twenty-five-mile ride.

The group left toward the back of the pack, with Layla somewhat nervous among so many horses. In the past, a horse had kicked her on the shin while riding in a group and the memory lingered. She'd had to go to the emergency room, where they had diagnosed her with a painful bone bruise. This event always surfaced in her mind whenever she felt trapped in a large group of riders.

In general, Layla's luck with horses hadn't been great. She had fallen off multiple times and seemed to attract random horse accidents. It was almost a guarantee that Flash would not alleviate any of her fears, but Flash had been so shocked to find Layla on his back and Kyla riding next to him on a different horse that he forgot to be his usual obnoxious self and carried Layla through the ride safely. This gave Layla a big confidence boost. Since she and Flash had survived their first ride together so well, Layla asked Natalie if she could ride Flash again the next day while Natalie rode Coco.

When Layla woke up the next day, she changed her mind and decided she didn't want to ride again, after all. She was sore from the previous day's fifty-mile ride, and the adrenaline high of finishing her first endurance ride had worn off. Because she had agreed to ride and Adam had already left camp with the other children for the amusement park, Natalie told Layla that she needed to "suck it up and get on that horse!" To those watching, Natalie knew this tough-love method may have seemed a little harsh, but she had never believed in giving in to her children's whims. If they made a commitment to do something, they were required to fulfill it. Besides, she couldn't leave Layla at camp alone.

As it happened, Layla survived the second day just fine and could now tease Kyla that she had done *seventy-five* miles while she was still only eight years old! Kyla was happy for her sister but was surprised at how hard it was for her to see Layla riding Flash. She supposed it was only natural that she should find it strange to see someone else riding her pony, even her sister. But deep down, Kyla was worried that as Layla and Flash spent more time together he would come to love Kyla less.

She couldn't stand hearing people using their names together in the same sentence. It was supposed to be *Kyla* and Flash, not *Layla* and Flash. Riding Flash had given her a chance to shine, to feel important compared to the kid she was at school, who was either ignored or bullied. Having that taken away from her, and the uncertainty over whether she would be able to compete at Tevis that summer, weighed heavily on her. Flash had been hers for almost a third of her life. Now she felt as if he was slowly disappearing, and as that happened, she felt as if she was slowly disappearing too. She, Layla, Flash, and endurance riding had become inextricably entwined in a puzzle of self-worth and acceptance. Somehow, she needed to figure out who she was and who she wanted to become. She knew it was important that those things not be tied to something that could be taken away from her at any moment. She decided to discuss the situation with her father since he had always been a huge supporter of her journey with Flash. Kyla leaned on Adam for advice, and as usual he quelled her fears.

Adam could see his daughter's internal struggle. He knew this was a pivotal moment in her young life and that the only way for her to find clarity would be through a deeper understanding of her relationship with God.

"Trust in God, Kyla," he told her. "He will guide you on whatever path is meant for you, even if it's not the same one you see for yourself. Pray when you have doubts and listen for the answers. If you can feel the Holy Spirit surrounding you, you will know what your purpose is and who you are!"

Kyla thought about how being around her parents always comforted her, and how she could feel the Holy Spirit surrounding them. But somehow she couldn't always feel that herself, however hard she tried. It was hard for her to admit to herself, let alone to her parents, that her faith might be lacking.

"I know you can do anything you put your mind to, Kyla," Adam continued. "If riding in Tevis is what God has planned for you, it will happen, and I know you'll give it one hundred percent of your effort. I have faith in you."

Kyla took a deep breath. She knew from the teachings of the Church that he was right. She would do everything in her power to make it happen and leave the rest to God. God was the one thing that would never change. If she could lay all her doubts and all her frustrations at His feet, then she would never have to bear them alone. Besides, her father had faith in her, and that was all she needed to hear.

• • •

In May, Natalie took Layla and Flash to what had now become a regular ride for the Law family, the XP ride at Mount Carmel. They loved reconnecting with Annie and The Duck, and with the Tevis Cup now on their agenda, Natalie really wanted to discuss their upcoming plans with the Nicholsons. The ride came three weeks after Antelope Island, and they had planned to ride just one of the multiday ride due to other family commitments. Natalie was riding Brave, Kacey Oar was on her own horse—an Arabian that could be quite a handful—and Kyla was on a new horse called Prancy. Prancy was a pretty bay Saddlebred mare that the Law family had acquired from Shelah Wetter thinking she may work out as Kyla's future endurance horse. Natalie hoped Prancy would help soften the blow of handing Flash over to Layla.

Layla was not over her fear of group riding, and the start of an endurance ride can be challenging when a horse is hard to control from excitement. Natalie instructed Layla to tuck Flash in behind Brave so that Natalie could control the pace, but when the horses took off at the start, Layla was unable to hold Flash back. Flash darted around Brave and took off at a gallop, dodging past other horses and cutting them off at the turns, Layla flailing and screaming on his back all the while.

"I can't stop him!" she yelled to her mother. When Natalie shouted instructions for slowing Flash down, Layla screamed back in a panic, "It's not working! I can't do it!"

As Natalie chased after Layla, Kacey and Kyla chased after Natalie—as junior riders they were required to stay with their sponsor! Kyla was thinking to herself that Layla really should have practiced those one-rein stops, while Kacey was trying to control her own horse now amped up with all the excitement. Natalie was horrified at what was happening to Layla and equally mortified that the whole group was now flying past well-known and prestigious endurance riders as she tried to chase her daughter down, all the while trying not to add fuel to the fire and make Flash go even faster.

Many riders got to witness the show that morning, as Layla went twelve miles down the trail in this fashion.

Kevin Waters, a longtime endurance rider often in attendance at the XP rides, saw something small and dark bolt past him on the trail that day, a screaming little girl attached to it. Thankfully, he managed to pull Flash over and return the excited pony and the shaking eight-year-old to her mother, who gave them both a few minutes to regroup, stuck them behind Brave, and continued with the ride. Even doing the rest of the ride at a far more moderate pace, Layla came in sixth place.

CHAPTER 10

Gearing Up

"Heaven is under our feet, as well as over our heads."
—HENRY DAVID THOREAU

So many things would have to go perfectly for them to make it to the starting line at the Tevis Cup. As a junior rider, Kyla would have to ride with a sponsor, so it was imperative that not only Kyla and Flash make it to the start, but Natalie and Brave as well. Two horses meant double the chances of something going wrong. They could just feel the Tevis gremlins—those invisible little no-gooders who stole Tevis dreams from unsuspecting entrants—rubbing their hands together in glee.

At most endurance rides a junior can find an alternative sponsor to ride with should their original sponsor be pulled. There were always a handful of experienced riders who would be happy to help a junior rider get through a ride. The sport of endurance is well known for the generous spirit of its community. But Tevis was different. The expense and training devoted to this ride meant it would be much harder to find someone willing to risk their own ride to assist a stray junior rider. So, if Natalie didn't make it to the start, it was unlikely that Kyla would either. To succeed, everything would have to go almost perfectly from the moment Flash's entry was submitted, to the moment they crossed the finish line in Auburn. The race against time continued, its ticking getting louder.

Natalie didn't tell Kyla how popular Flash was becoming on Facebook. She didn't want Kyla to feel the added pressure of a thousand eyes watching her and Flash as they trained for the event. Everyone following their journey was rooting for them to make it to the Tevis Cup starting line, which meant that on race day itself, the pair of them would be watched across the world as they took on the challenge of the Tevis trail.

Several things were in their favor. The Laws lived and trained on some of the most challenging trails that Southern Utah had to offer; trails that were rugged and technical, and offered stunning scenery. Most of the miles they put on Flash had him running loose beside Natalie as she trained Brave so that Flash would still have plenty of long training miles even with Kyla in school. The horses needed plenty of long, slow miles on steep terrain to condition for Tevis. Conditioning a horse for endurance is very similar to a human training for an ultramarathon. In fact, the Western States Trail Run, which takes place on an almost identical one-hundred-mile course as the Tevis Cup, was started by an endurance rider whose horse showed up lame at the start of Tevis. In 1974 Gordy Ainsleigh was given permission to take on the challenge by foot and completed the one-hundred-mile course within the twenty-four-hour time limit, thereby birthing a whole new endurance event. Since then, the run happens every year about a month before the ride, and the two events work hand in hand to preserve and maintain the trail.

Another advantage for Natalie and Kyla was their proximity to the XP rides. Once the decision to ride Tevis had been made, The Duck and Annie Nicholson jumped in as both mentors and cheerleaders to help the little girl and her Hackney pony make their goal.

Natalie consulted The Duck and many other experts about her main concern with Flash. Flash had never worn hoof protection. He was blessed with very tough feet, and his feet had only become tougher as he covered more terrain in his training. However, one of the Tevis rules was that every horse had to have hoof protection at the ride, and while Natalie could write an appeal to go barefoot, she thought it might be prudent to stick to the rules. Even horses that were used to going barefoot would find the conditions at this ride challenging, and even the most hard-core barefoot advocates found themselves gluing on boots for the Tevis trail. So Natalie began researching the best way to overcome this challenge for Flash, with his exceptionally tiny hooves.

Natalie contacted just about everyone in the hoof protection world that she knew of, and an army of people willingly took up the challenge of helping Flash. Natalie spoke with Dave Rabe, Christoph Schork, Tennessee Lane, and The Duck about the possibility of using a glue on boot by a company called Easyboots. Many horses had successfully completed Tevis with this product, but after trying every size possible, none were small enough for Flash. Tennessee Lane and the The Southern Colorado Endurance Club really got behind their efforts and said whatever route the Laws chose they would cover the cost of Flash's hoof protection; another fine example of endurance community selflessness. A man by the name of Mark Lindsey was even willing to design a specific shoe just for Flash, but the time it would take to design wouldn't leave enough room to test the boots before the big ride, and Natalie wasn't willing to take that risk.

Finally, Stacy Pratt from Heartland Scoot Boots sent Natalie several boxes of boots in assorted sizes specifically designed for miniature horses, and it looked as if there were some that might work. The boots would need to be modified so they could be glued onto his hoof rather than strapped on, but at least they now had a product that held some promise. By working closely with Stacy, they finally came up with a modified product that could do the job. Stacy called them Scoot Skins.

To test them out, Natalie needed Kyla to put Flash through a multi-day ride to see how they fared. She chose the City of Rocks Pioneer Endurance Ride, which took place over three days at the beginning of June, seven weeks before the start date of the 2021 Tevis Cup. The next challenge was to find someone who had the skill level to shape and prep Flash's hooves before the boots could be applied. There was no one geographically close enough to the Laws with experience in gluing on boots to help Natalie. But between her and her farrier, Don Stewart, they Googled and YouTubed the process until they felt confident that, between them, they could get the job done. Two days before the City of Rocks ride, they tied Flash up to a post in the barn, gave him a bucket of feed to distract him, and got to work. Don did the shaping and prep work, and Natalie glued on the boots. At last, Flash stood there with his first full set of boots custom fit and wrapped around his little hooves, offering all the hoof protection he had never really needed!

It was important to make sure that Flash could still comfortably handle Kyla's weight and height, so Kyla would ride Flash on the fifty-mile ride on day one and day two, giving them a total of one hundred miles over the course of the two days. Layla would ride Flash in the twenty-five-mile ride on day three, when he would theoretically be calmer. This would top off his fitness level with a shorter ride and a lighter rider. Kyla was thrilled to be sitting astride her pony again. He was proudly sporting his new set of boots, his Pandora saddle, and his green biothane bridle. If he could get through the next two days with Kyla without any undue strain, they would be ready for Tevis.

Layla had found her own kind of fame as the young girl on the runaway pony at Mount Carmel. Dave Rabe, Hall of Fame endurance rider with 75,000 competitive miles to his name, spotted the Law family the night before the City of Rocks ride began. He decided that he needed to warn the Law family about the dangers of riding a wild pony at the Tevis Cup. He approached Natalie in ride camp, introduced himself, and reminded her that the Tevis Cup is a tough and challenging ride. If Flash bolted or ran through other riders and horses, he could endanger not only himself but others as well. It was a valid point, and Dave's concerns were justified; the Tevis Cup was no place for a feral pony and a scared young girl. Natalie reassured Dave that it would be the older and more experienced Kyla riding Flash at Tevis and not Layla. She assured Dave that Kyla had the knowledge and experience to control Flash and that the bond the two had developed over the last four years would carry them through. She hoped her assessment of the situation was correct.

The next day, Dave saw Kyla and Flash out on the trails and realized that with this pair there was nothing to worry about. Flash floated along the trails, thrilled to have Kyla on his back once again, and Kyla was back in her happy place. Dave enjoyed witnessing the unique bond they shared and was confident that the two of them could safely navigate the challenges of the Tevis trail.

Dave Rabe is one of the nicest men in the endurance community and obviously knows a thing or two about endurance riding. He made a mental note to seek Kyla and Flash out at the Tevis Cup ride camp and wish them luck and success with their endeavors.

The City of Rocks ride was a huge success. They rode a little more conservatively than usual, as they wanted Flash to complete all three days of the ride. They needn't have worried. Flash carried Kyla to a sixth and twenty-sixth place finish the first two days, and Layla to an eleventh place finish on the Limited Distance ride on day three. He made it all look easy. Flash carried Kyla with the same ease and enthusiasm he always had, and with a few minor adjustments to the tack, both Kyla and Natalie felt that he would be able to carry Kyla one hundred miles across the Sierras in a few short weeks.

Their only dilemma was an issue with the boots. The first boot fell off by mile five, and by thirty miles into the ride Flash had lost all four of them. He finished the rest of the ride happily barefoot and perfectly sound. Natalie was sure that it had been an application issue and that there was no reason the boots couldn't work for them at Tevis, especially if she could find someone with more experience to put them on.

• • •

Now that it was confirmed Kyla would be able to attempt the Tevis Cup ride on Flash, it was time to finish putting all the details in place to ensure a successful ride. Natalie and Kyla realized their dreams were really happening, and they could hardly contain their excitement. After four years and a roller coaster of experiences and emotions, Kyla would have her final ride on Flash at the world-famous Tevis Cup.

Her race against time would now become a race against the twenty-four-hour finish time and the cutoffs that were established at various checkpoints along the way. Natalie felt blessed to be able to experience this with Kyla. Not only because of their history of riding together, but also because she knew as her children got older and more independent she may not always have these precious times with them. Kyla was now a teenager, and Natalie had no idea how the years ahead with her would go. She had laid a strong foundation for her daughter based on faith, the chance to learn and grow from her own mistakes, and the myriad of life experiences that endurance riding had offered them both over the last two years. Despite that, Natalie knew that doing this ride across the Sierras with her daughter would be a pivotal moment in their relationships. If they could overcome the challenges of the mountains, Natalie knew that she and her daughter would have a life-changing experience together.

PART II
The Tevis Cup

CHAPTER 11

Rattled Nerves

*"Sometimes the questions are complicated,
and the answers are simple."*

—DR. SEUSS

With the final ride before Tevis completed, Natalie needed to finish making plans for their upcoming adventure. One of the most important decisions included securing a crew who could be there for them every step of the way. The Tevis Cup started in one place and finished one hundred miles away in another.

A point-to-point ride, rather than one that loops back to ride camp, creates logistical challenges that other rides don't have, such as moving the rig from the start to the finish, and often to other points in between. While much of crewing consists of "hurry up and wait," a crew that works like a well-oiled machine can be very beneficial to helping a horse and rider get through the checkpoints efficiently. There's a knack to crewing a large event like the Tevis Cup, and experience plays a big part in that. Finding a crew that had either ridden or crewed Tevis previously would be the ideal scenario, especially as it was both Natalie and Kyla's first time there.

Natalie knew that having a good crew could improve their chances of finishing the ride. Before Tevis was seriously on her radar, Natalie had asked Shelah, "If I ever go to Tevis, will you crew for me?" Of course, Shelah had said yes (not knowing when or if the moment would actually come about) and now Natalie intended to hold her to that promise. Shelah and Natalie put their heads together and came up with a plan. Both believed in being well prepared and then getting on with the job while not stressing out over the small things. The other benefit to having Shelah on board was that Kyla and Shelah were close, and Shelah knew Flash so well that she would be a huge resource during the ride.

With their main crew member on board, Natalie and Kyla began choosing the rest of the team. They asked Kacey Oar, the junior rider who had ridden with them many times. Kacey was an accomplished equestrian, and it would be nice for Kyla to have someone closer to her own age there to help. She was also young and strong, which was a benefit since crewing often involved schlepping heavy objects from one place to another.

Next on the list was Adam Law. Since Brave had been purchased for Adam, it seemed appropriate that he step up and care for his horse while Natalie had the fun job of riding him. Adam was severely allergic to both hay and horses, but he wouldn't miss the chance to offer his support and do whatever he could to help his wife and daughter. Adam had been Kyla's biggest advocate leading up to the ride, and both Kyla and Natalie would appreciate his calming presence at the vet checks.

To round out the crew Natalie invited her parents, James and Wynona Mayer. When Natalie was growing up, her parents had constantly reminded her that she could achieve whatever she put her mind to. They had given their unwavering support to their daughter and granddaughter in this latest venture and were excited to help in whatever capacity they could.

With Flash's social media following growing daily, Natalie could have put out a plea for help and attracted some experienced crew to help them that year. But as usual, she had her own way of doing things. In her gut she knew that familiar faces who knew them and their horses would be most important for her and Kyla that day. Shelah was an experienced equestrian with many endurance rides under her belt, and although she had never ridden in the Tevis Cup she could adapt and use her knowledge to lead their crew better than most.

Out of the five crew members, the two riders, and the two horses on Team Law, not one of them had ever been to Tevis before, either to crew, volunteer, or spectate. Natalie hoped that a combination of good preparation, beginner's luck, and prayer would suffice to get their team successfully through the race.

• • •

The week of the Tevis Cup was almost upon them. Natalie and Kyla spent several days prepping supplies and packing them into the horse trailer. It was a monumental task. For some reason, getting ready for Tevis seemed far more demanding of both their time and organizational skills than any previous ride. They packed their crew bags with everything they could think of and tagged them for the appropriate vet check. They knew that everything they needed for the first major vet check at Robinson Flat would have to be packed in and out of camp by her crew, and they had heard from the Tevis organizers that there would be limited space available at Robinson this year due to campground closures. They needed to make sure they had everything they needed, and nothing they didn't.

Next, they organized who would be at each vet check and made sure everyone had a list of each team member's phone numbers so they could stay in touch throughout the ride. They packed blankets for the horses, grain, hay, rump rugs, medical supplies, flashlights and lanterns, bedding for the night before the ride, cots, as well as clothing, toiletries, and everything the horses and humans would need. Months before, Natalie had booked an Airbnb in Auburn, very close to the Tevis office as it turned out, and they would use this as their base for the week. Natalie had talked to all the mentors she had found along her endurance journey to make sure she was as prepared as possible for this ride. She had written plans, made extensive lists, and had gone through everything in her mind a hundred times.

Kyla didn't know much about the history of Tevis or why it was so special. To her, it was important because it was the big finale to her endurance career with Flash. She wasn't as concerned with the trail as she was with her ability to get through the ride. Even though everything had gone well at the City of Rocks, she was still concerned that Flash would struggle to carry her that distance. While multi-day rides are wonderful for conditioning a horse, a one-hundred-mile ride in under twenty-four hours was a vastly different challenge, especially one with an elevation gain of 14,800 feet and a loss of 22,800 feet. That was an awful lot of climbs and descents for Flash to carry her over. Kyla hadn't ridden as much as she had the previous year, and she wondered if her growing body would handle the challenge as easily as it once had. She knew the only way to find the answer to that question was to do the ride and see what happened.

• • •

The plan was for Natalie to drive the truck, pulling the horse trailer from Utah to California, and take Kyla, Kacey, and Natalie's mother, Wynona. Shelah would fly into Sacramento airport from Washington. Adam and his father-in-law, James, who had a private plane, would fly into Sacramento the Thursday before the ride. Once they landed, they would locate Shelah and drive up together to meet the others in Auburn.

Natalie split the long drive into two days so it would be less taxing on the horses. They both happily jumped into the trailer the day they left; they were used to being trailered to rides and endurance events and were unaware that this trip would take them to the most important adventure of their lives.

By doing the bulk of the drive on the first day—seven hours to Yerington, Nevada—they would only have three hours to go on day two to reach Auburn. The owners of the Airbnb in Yerington were more than accommodating and happy to have the horses tied to the trailer. This close to Tevis, it was important to keep their horses close by, and preferably bubble-wrapped, to avoid any injuries on the journey there.

The Laws and their crew arrived in Auburn on Wednesday, July 20, 2021, and got the horses settled into their stalls at the Gold Country Fairgrounds, where they could relax after the long journey. Kyla suddenly realized that this ride was a much bigger deal than she thought. As they had entered the town of Auburn, enormous banners welcomed the Tevis riders, and pulling into the fairgrounds Kyla began to get her first case of Tevis nerves. Natalie tied a brown paper bag to the stall door asking people to leave messages of encouragement for Kyla. Since Kyla was unaware of the number of people following Flash on social media, Natalie thought the notes would be a pleasant surprise for her to read.

After checking into their Airbnb, the girls enjoyed looking around the town of Auburn with its historic main street, stores, and restaurants. Auburn was a fascinating place that sprung up in the gold mining era. It was incorporated in the year 1888, and the whole town is now registered as a California historic landmark. In 2003 the Auburn city council adopted a proclamation that named Auburn the Endurance Capital of the World. Considering it's the home of the Tevis Cup, the Western States Endurance Run, the Auburn Triathlon, and the Auburn Century, the UTMB Canyons Endurance Runs, and numerous other endurance events, the title is well deserved.

Arriving at the Gold Country Fairgrounds early is like arriving at a football stadium a week before the big game. The fairgrounds are empty, and it's hard to find anyone if you have questions. It's hard to believe that it will soon transform into a small village as one by one the rigs arrive and the stalls begin to fill with some of the leanest and fittest equines in the United States. The horses, mostly regal Arabians, step out of their trailers, heads and tails held high, nostrils snorting as they assess their new surroundings. People scurry around organizing everything they will need for their brief time at the fairgrounds before heading up to the ride camp at Robie Park for the start. They nod to strangers, knowing they shared a version of the same challenging journey taken to get there, and they greet those they know, talking excitedly about finally being here, the mecca of the endurance world.

Trucks arrive from Echo Valley Ranch Feed, the local feed store sponsor, bringing shavings for the stalls and hay for the horses. Greg Kimler, the owner, is an avid endurance rider himself with four Tevis completions, and Echo Valley Ranch Feed has been an important sponsor of the Tevis Cup since the late 1980s. As the day grows closer, things get busier, the excited buzz in the air increasing with each passing day.

Brave and Flash certainly knew how to cause a stir. Word spread around the barns that a tiny Hackney pony was in stall 18 in Barn 1, happily munching on his hay and acting like he deserved to be hanging with the big boys! He was being carefully watched over by his friend in the stall next door—a tall, powerful, and impressive Saddlebred. Natalie and Kyla enjoyed everyone's curiosity and proudly showed Flash to anyone who asked. They were aware that at a ride of this caliber both horses were representatives of their breed.

On Thursday, Wynona dropped Natalie, Kyla, and the horses off at a turnoff where they could connect with the Tevis trail and ride the last few miles to the finish. It would help to see the course in daylight, as they would undoubtedly be riding this section in the middle of the night at the actual ride. By riding it now, the horses would recognize this section of trail and know they were close to finishing when they reached that point on race day. Seeing the trail now might give them the final burst of energy they would need after ninety-six miles to make it to the finish line.

If only horses could be bubble wrapped and protected until the point when the ride began on Saturday! Even a light workout on the trail was a risk for the horses, but then so was standing in the stall or being tied to the trailer. An accident could happen anywhere and sometimes was impossible to avoid. Natalie and Kyla set off on their training ride, hoping it would be both uneventful and informative.

The ride was going smoothly. Beautiful views of the canyon carved by the American River surrounded them. They were day dreaming of what they hoped would be a spectacular finish on Sunday morning when suddenly Kyla let out a scream. She and Flash were in front, flying along the trail at a fast clip with Natalie and Brave following close behind. As they rounded a corner, Kyla saw a large snake crossing the trail right in front of her.

"Mom, a snake! Noooooo!"

Kyla hadn't noticed the rattlesnake crossing the trail until it was too late. She tried to stop Flash but to no avail. The snake panicked. Flash panicked. Kyla and Natalie panicked. When Flash realized the snake was squirming between his legs, he spun in circles, confusing the reptile who must have momentarily forgotten how to strike in the cloud of dust. Flash bolted from the scene, and Kyla managed to do a one-rein stop on the narrow trail as she dangled off the side of the saddle.

When Kyla finally caught her breath and Flash stopped trying to bolt even farther away, she immediately dismounted the trembling pony to make sure he had not been bitten.

"Easy, easy," she told the trembling pony. She hadn't seen him this scared since she first met him.

"Mom, I can't make him stand still so I can check his legs!"

Natalie was already off Brave and had led him over to where Flash was circling Kyla, his tail tucked beneath him.

"Easy, Flash!" Natalie said. "Easy there, let me look at you. There's a good boy."

Flash stood still as close to Brave as he could get, no doubt hoping the larger horse could protect him from any other trail monsters.

"Stay by his head while I check his legs and belly," Natalie ordered Kyla, who stood there shaking almost as much as Flash. She'd had visions of getting dumped on the trail right on top of the snake, and for once she was happy that Flash's go-to move was to run fast!

"Is he okay?" Kyla asked, stroking his muzzle as Flash finally blew out his nostrils and visibly relaxed.

"Yes, I think so," Natalie replied. "He seems fine. There's no sign of a bite. He was just scared."

"Are we going to run into snakes on the trail at night?" Kyla asked nervously. "How will we see them? What if we get bitten out on the trail and we're too far away from anyone to get help?"

Natalie knew that if she didn't give her daughter some perspective about the incident now, her fear could take over on the day of the ride and ruin her whole experience.

"Things do happen on the trail, Kyla, but this was unusual. Think how many people ride on this trail and never see a snake, or a mountain lion or bear for that matter. It was just an unfortunate incident, but we are all fine. Let's not make more of it than it was. Time to get back on and finish the ride!"

The snake had recovered and appeared to have left the scene, presumably relieved to have survived the experience himself. Once Kyla was over the immediate shock of the incident, she realized how close Flash had come to possibly being unable to start the race. As small as he was, Kyla didn't know if he would have even survived a rattlesnake bite, although she suspected it would take more than that to take down a pony as tenacious as Flash. She had been concerned about cougars and steep drop-offs during the ride but had never thought about the dangers of rattlesnakes on the trail. Despite Natalie's words, Kyla was terrified of running into more snakes and found it difficult to put the incident behind her. What on earth had she gotten herself and Flash into?

They returned to the fairgrounds without further incident. Once the horses were settled in for the night, the group made their way to the Airbnb to go over some last-minute plans before heading up to Robie Park the next day. The rest of the crew had arrived safely, although Shelah was not feeling well at all. She had become sick a couple of days earlier, but as the crew leader she wasn't about to leave Natalie and Kyla without her help. She was hoping she would feel better by the start of the ride. Natalie was thankful that Shelah had decided to come. It would have been almost impossible to manage without her.

Shelah visited the horses at the barn and was pleased to see how fit and healthy they both looked. She gave Natalie and Kyla credit for bringing the horses along with a lot of slow and steady training miles, and for using The Duck's XP rides as the perfect training ground for the challenge they were about to undertake. Shelah felt confident that, barring any unforeseen happenings, such as what they now referred to as "the snake incident," the horses had as good a chance as any for a successful ride.

• • •

Friday morning the group arrived at Robie Park, where they would camp overnight. Robie Park was a large clearing approximately twenty miles off Highway 69. For a few brief days each year it turned into the bustling Tevis Cup ride camp. The camp gradually filled with rigs, trucks, trailers, and motor homes, as well as food vendors and booths, and the local bear population who came to picnic there every year, knowing they could easily steal the mash from the horses' feed buckets when no one was looking.

Once they arrived, Team Law unloaded the trailer and started organizing. Natalie panicked when she realized that, despite all her preparations, she had left the horses' blankets behind in Auburn. The horses had been body clipped to help them deal with the summer heat in the desert, but here the night temperatures dropped well below what they were used to and the blankets were a necessity. Natalie's dad came to their rescue and offered to do the four-hour round trip drive back to Auburn to retrieve them while Kyla and Natalie finished setting up their camp and vetting the horses in.

Although Flash was used to running free in ride camp, Natalie knew that at Robie Park they would need to contain him. She had brought four lightweight panels that fit together to make a 7 by 7 stall to put him in next to Brave, who would be tied to the trailer. When Kyla led Flash into the little coral they had to laugh at the look on his face. He could not fathom why on earth they would put him in such a thing—he would much rather have been running around exploring.

Flash caused quite the scene as he and Brave walked through camp to the vetting-in area. Even those who had been following Flash on Facebook were surprised at how tiny he was in real life. Even for a Hackney pony Flash was small, and since Kyla had grown several inches in the last couple of years, she looked tall standing next to him. It was obvious that if Tevis had been canceled this year there was no way that Flash would have been able to carry her a year later. This was their one and only chance.

The 2021 Tevis cup had been a tough one for organizers. They initially received three hundred entries, many of which were withdrawn before the event. Many riders had not been able to condition their horses adequately with all the ride cancellations still taking place. But Chuck Stalley and his team of organizers decided that, so long as they had one hundred participants, the ride would go on. Thankfully one hundred and thirty-three teams were ready to vet in that Friday before the ride.

The next challenge for organizers was that the first one-hour vet check at Robinson Flat would need to be contained to a much smaller area than usual. Rather than spreading out across a meadow full of trees offering shade and plenty of space for a crew to lay everything out for their horse and rider, Robinson Flat was partially closed by the forest service. So this year the space would be limited to the dirt road coming off the trail and approaching the meadow.

The vets would be set up near the entrance to the campground from the main access road. With the lower-than-usual number of entries, Chuck Stalley hoped that everyone would cooperate with each other and make it work.

The more immediate concern for organizers was a wildfire burning south of Lake Tahoe. The Tamarack Fire had been raging since July 4 and had grown to more than 100,000 acres. The west-to-east winds had been driving the smoke away from Robie Park until a few days before the ride. But now the wind had shifted, and a strong smell of smoke hung in the air as competitors arrived to check in. Ride management had serious concerns about air quality, and although it was unlikely the fire itself would immediately threaten the area, they would feel a lot more comfortable once they had moved everyone out of the high country. These issues compounded the stress of running such a complicated event. Chuck Stalley knew from experience that the day of the ride was bound to bring its own challenges; it always did.

One thing Chuck was not too concerned about was the junior rider, Kyla Law, and her Hackney pony, Flash. Chuck had received a phone call from Dave "The Duck" Nicholson informing him that Kyla and Flash were the real deal and could handle themselves just fine the day of the ride. With such glowing praise from The Duck, Chuck was curious to see just how well Kyla and Flash would navigate the one hundred miles of the Western States Trail.

• • •

The initial vet check was held in a large flat area in the middle of Robie Park. Large boulders a few feet apart defined the space, and observers could lean or sit on them to watch the horses vetting in. This was one of the few parts of an endurance ride that was spectator friendly, and many curious onlookers enjoyed watching the fit horses trotting out for the vets.

There were multiple vets available to check in the field of horses that afternoon. As Kyla led Flash up to them an argument erupted as to which vet would have the enjoyment of vetting him in. It was such an unusual circumstance to have a horse this small at Tevis, and each one wanted to be a part of his adventure. Some lucky vet won, and Flash stepped forward to be examined. By this time, he was quite used to being vetted in at rides. That didn't mean he liked it, but with Kyla by his side he allowed the vets to listen to his gut sounds and check his muscle tone, mucus membranes, and capillary and jugular refill. They also checked for any tack galls or wounds that would be noted on his card. The vet listened to Flash's heart rate and made a note of it on his vet card.

At subsequent vet checks the horses' heart rates would not just be checked, but they would also have to pass a CRI—a cardiac recovery index—which indicated a horse's fitness and how well it was tolerating the stress of the endurance ride. The vet writes down the initial heart rate at the beginning of the exam and then records the next heart rate sixty seconds later, after the horse has trotted out to an orange cone and back. If the second recorded heart rate is higher than the first by more than a few beats, there could be cause for concern. Throughout the race on Saturday, each horse would be examined repeatedly to make sure they were tolerating the competition without any undue physical stress.

While less than fifty percent of the starting teams finish Tevis, there are rarely any serious incidents on the trail. Most "pulls" during the race are due to minor lameness issues, issues with the rider, such as heat exhaustion or vertigo, or a metabolic issue with the horse that can be resolved with intravenous fluids. If a horse struggles metabolically during the ride they are immediately stabilized and trailered back to the fairgrounds where treatment vets are on standby to help them recover. There is an inherent risk, however, of participating in a race that takes place across a wilderness with areas that are inaccessible. Horse and rider are in most danger there. In very rare instances, horses have gone over the side of a cliff, and these require a dramatic helicopter rescue. Despite the infrequency of these accidents, they still tend to hover in the back of a rider's imagination—or at the front of it if they happen to be riding along part of the trail that hangs on the edge of a cliff with a thousand-foot drop-off on one side. These dangers are often a deterrent for endurance riders who may otherwise attempt the ride.

The number of strong finishers and low instances of any significant injuries during the Tevis Cup and the hundreds of endurance rides across the country attests to the fact that a well-managed horse is perfectly capable of covering these distances, and many can be seen prancing around their paddocks the next day. Part of the success of endurance riding as a sport are the rules and regulations that protect the horse during such an event, and the vetting procedure is thorough and consistent, with the vets at Tevis being the most experienced in their field.

When Kyla trotted Flash out to the orange cone 150 feet away, turned, and trotted back to the vet, the crowd exploded. The dark little pony with so much attitude held his tail high, kicked up his heels, and put on a show for all those watching. Kyla had to run fast to keep up with him, and Flash made sure that if anyone had yet to fall in love with him that day, this would seal the deal. He looked spectacular. The vet smiled and gave him all A's on his vet card. His heart rate was an impressive 32 beats per minute. If Flash could survive the night without injury, at 5 a.m. the next morning he would be standing at the starting line of the Tevis Cup.

Flash had come a long way from the trembling, wild little pony that Kyla first met four years ago. No one would have suspected that the brave pony putting on such a fine show for the crowds at Robie Park had once been filled with fear, or that the girl so proudly running alongside him had had her confidence smashed to pieces by bullies. This was their moment to shine, and shine they did.

Natalie then trotted Brave out—the largest horse at the event that year—and they all breathed a sigh of relief when he, too, passed the vet check with flying colors. It seemed as if the teams were really going to get the chance to compete together in the world's most famous endurance race. The largest horse and the smallest horse. The mother and daughter team. The completely inexperienced crew. Could they really do it? As Natalie and Kyla headed back to the trailer, Natalie looked across at her daughter with one thought: *Well, why not?*

CHAPTER 12

Let the Games Begin

"I could never resist the call of the trail."

—BUFFALO BILL CODY

It was time for Flash to have his boots professionally glued on by John Perry. John had agreed to meet the Laws at Robie Park on Friday afternoon and spend the two hours or so that it would take to properly glue on Flash's custom Scoot Skins.

John was also riding the next day on his eight-year-old chestnut gelding, appropriately named Follow Your Dream. He had a long list of things he needed to organize for his own ride and was anxious to get the boots on the pony so he could get back to his own horse. However organized participants think they are headed into Tevis, there always seem to be more things to do, right up to the last minute. When John saw Flash standing quietly by the trailer looking so adorable, he was glad he had agreed to help the young girl with her cute little Hackney pony. He put a smile on his face and walked over to introduce himself to the Law family and their crew. The poor man had no idea what he was in for!

By this time, Flash had progressed from a scared little pony to one who thought he should probably rule the world—no, the universe. He had an opinion about everything, and he had a very definite opinion about letting this strange man fuss around with his feet to get those annoying boots on again. Flash fussed, moved around, snorted his disapproval, and at one point reared and almost went over John's shoulder. The ground was dusty, the temperatures were warm, the pony was downright rotten, but after three difficult hours John had secured all four boots to Flash's hooves.

"I don't know about that last one, Natalie," John said as he stepped back to survey his handiwork. He was breathing heavily, and it was the first time he had hoofprints on his shirt from working on a horse.

"I wouldn't place a bet on that one staying on, but it's the best I can do, considering the circumstances."

John glanced at Flash for a moment, and Flash stared back, ready for another round if the farrier came near him again.

Natalie cringed inwardly but tried to keep her voice light as she said, "I'm sure he was just trying to give you a hug, John!" Seeing that John wasn't buying it for a second, she added, "An 11'2" hand pony about to take on the Tevis Cup needs to have some fire in his soul, right?"

John reluctantly agreed and left feeling like even riding the Tevis trail had to be easier than what he had just gone through.

• • •

Kyla hadn't realized how many people knew about Flash and didn't expect to draw so much attention from those in camp. Dave Rabe had made a point of finding them and was happy to see they had indeed made it to the start of Tevis. He felt as if he now had a vested interest in their success. Natalie and Kyla were thrilled he had taken time out of his day to seek them out and wish them well.

Kacey and Kyla took Flash for a walk around camp, and everywhere they went people would come up to them with questions and comments: "Is that Flash?" "Look at how small that pony is!" "I can't believe you're doing Tevis on him!"

While people were genuinely curious and always supportive, the comments opened Kyla's eyes to the enormity of what she and Flash were about to attempt the next day, and with so much attention on Flash, Kacey could see that Kyla felt a little left out and was probably thinking, *What about me? This is my big moment, too!*

Kyla had reluctantly attended three pre-ride meetings that afternoon. There was a first-time riders meeting, a junior riders meeting, and then the main pre-ride meeting that everyone attended. It wasn't that she wasn't interested in what they had to say, but with each successive meeting Kyla's anxiety grew. This certainly didn't feel like any ride she had done so far. The vetting was far more official, with multiple vets all wearing their yellow safety vests marked TEVIS VET in large black letters on the back. The vendors and crowds gave ride camp an almost festive atmosphere, and Kyla watched as 133 competitors all mingled and strutted their fit and successful endurance horses around camp. This was a smaller field of competitors than usual, but there was still a lot more going on here than at the ride camps she was used to, especially when compared to the laid-back atmosphere that permeated the XP rides they regularly attended.

Kyla was intimidated. She internalized her anxiety, becoming quiet and then defensive in her responses to questions. Her family watched her silent meltdown and worried that she would be too overwhelmed to sleep, or even to ride the next day. Kyla's anxiety and nerves made her stomach queasy, so she didn't want to eat. She knew she needed to keep her energy up and feed her body for the task ahead, but she still resisted when Natalie and Adam insisted that she eat something, anything, knowing she needed the sustenance, until she finally choked down half a hamburger.

Riding in the Tevis Cup was nerve-wracking even for the adult participants. Whether it was their first or tenth time, competitors had the hardest time controlling pre-ride jitters. All the riders in camp were trying to distract themselves by running through their last-minute checklists, meeting with their crews, hand-walking their horses one last time, and talking with fellow endurance riders to get any last-minute advice. For a girl who had only just turned thirteen, and who had only just realized the extent of what she was about to attempt, the anxiety threatened to take over and ruin her whole experience.

Kacey saw that Kyla was struggling and pulled her aside.

"How are you feeling, Kyla? Don't stress out now! You're here! You're about to do the Tevis Cup!"

Kacey realized maybe that hadn't been the best thing to say as Kyla struggled to hold back her tears.

"What if I can't do it, Kacey? What if I haven't ridden enough lately, or my knees hurt too much for me to continue? Look how many people are following us, expecting me to help Flash finish this ride. I didn't realize it would be like this!"

All Kacey could do was reassure her friend and let her know that she would be there at the vet checks, waiting for her and ready to help with whatever Kyla needed.

"I know you can do it, Kyla! You and Flash can both do this! Just relax, and don't forget to breathe!"

At least that had put a smile on Kyla's worried face, if only for a second or two.

• • •

At the main ride meeting in front of the Barseleau pavilion, Chuck Stalley and his team gave up-to-date information on trail conditions and what riders could expect the next day. There would be a 5 a.m. controlled start and horses had been assigned to either Pen 1 or Pen 2—designated areas by the side of the dirt road that led to the entrance of the trail delineated by bright yellow caution tape. They would wait at these pens until cleared to start. Pen 1 would contain those horses who had qualified based on prior Tevis completions and their overall ride record. Those in Pen 1 would be moving down the trail at a faster pace than those in Pen 2 where Natalie and Kyla would start, and would almost certainly have goals in mind regarding placement for the ride. Most riders in Pen 2 would be happy to just finish within the twenty-four-hour time limit. A controlled start meant that in the darkness of the morning the horses would follow an experienced horse and rider for a certain distance at a walk before being released to move out at whatever pace they chose.

Natalie particularly appreciated Kathie Perry's advice. A long-time endurance rider and Tevis committee member with twenty-four Tevis finishers of her own, Kathie shared that it was important not to take too much time at the stops along the way, wasting valuable time that could make the difference between a completion and being overtime. She quoted the famous words of Dr. Matthew Mackay-Smith, an accomplished endurance rider, veterinarian, and member of the AERC Hall of Fame: "Never hurry, never tarry." These words were burned into the brains of so many in the endurance community that they had become a Tevis mantra of sorts. Hearing Kathie remind everyone of these words at the ride meeting gave Natalie something to focus on throughout the ride. *Don't push too hard, don't waste time, keep moving forward.*

That evening, Natalie and Kyla set up their air bed in the back of the horse trailer. They didn't have a living-quarters trailer or motor home like some other riders and were taking a more minimalist approach. Kacey and poor Shelah, who was still feeling sick, were sleeping in a tent nearby. Adam and Natalie's parents had returned to the Airbnb in Auburn for the night and would head out early the next morning to the Robinson Flat vet check.

Kyla went to bed that night with a thousand things running through her young mind. Natalie could tell Kyla wouldn't be able to fall asleep in her current state. The day was catching up with her, and the pressure had continued to build. It was a lot for a young girl to process. Kyla leaned on her mother for support, and Natalie responded by talking to her calmly about how they were just going to get up in the morning and go on a nice ride through the mountains together, just like they did at home. Natalie reminded Kyla that everyone there was feeling the Tevis jitters, especially those attempting the ride for the first time.

Natalie held her daughter close and they prayed together. They thanked God for the opportunity of taking up this challenge and for the magnificent horses He had blessed them with. They prayed that their horses would stay sound and that they would arrive in Auburn safely. They asked that they be given the chance to watch the sun rise and set together as they rode along the trail, but mostly that God would allow them to recognize the beauty in everything the journey would offer them, whether it be the glorious sights they would see, or the deepening of their bond with each other and with their horses. Kyla felt the comforting presence of the Spirit around her and felt a subtle but important shift in her mind. By the time they were done praying, Kyla felt the tension leave her. She was ready to lay down and get some much-needed rest.

Unfortunately, the air mattress sprung a slow leak, and the pair spent most of the next few hours trying to get comfortable. Kyla started to get a little congested, and her breathing became labored.

Natalie hoped that it was just allergies and would not develop into anything worse. She hoped that Covid was not going to hijack their ride experience again. At 3:30 a.m., after a restless night tossing and turning, Natalie gave up trying to sleep and rose in the darkness to check on the horses. She dressed in the clothes she had laid out the night before, knowing she would be in them for many long hours and miles that day. She fed the horses and then gently shook Kyla awake and told her it was time to get ready.

The forest around them was quiet. Other than the gentle stirrings from those in nearby camps, there was an eerie stillness in the air; the calm before the storm. The smoke from the distant fires had settled around them, and although they couldn't see the haze in the darkness, they could smell the unsettling, insidious scent that clung to the forest and wrapped itself into their hair, their nostrils, and the manes and tails of the horses who were steadily munching on their breakfast. It was a strange world they had awoken to. Unknowns haunted their minds as they went about the business of getting ready for what was up ahead. Kyla's stomach was gurgling, but she still wasn't feeling hungry. Her body wanted to remain asleep even as her mind started to ponder what she was about to do. This was it. This was the Tevis Cup. It was time.

Shelah and Kacey groomed and tacked up the horses while Natalie encouraged Kyla to eat half a banana and drink some Ensure. They checked their saddlebags, making sure they had everything they would need for the next thirty-six miles to reach the Robinson Flat vet check. Kyla made sure her saddlebag had her goldfish crackers and her favorite types of candy: Chewys, SweeTARTS, Nerds Rope, and bite-sized Airheads. She had been allowed to choose whatever she wanted to carry for snacks, although Natalie hoped she would get some better sustenance at the vet checks later in the day.

Although the skies were still dark above them, it was time to mount up. The horses were being surprisingly cooperative, and maybe, like Kyla, they were taking it all in, sensing that this ride was different from the others. They began walking the horses toward the start, intending to let them have a final drink at the water tanks set up around camp before getting into Pen 2 for the start. To Natalie's disappointment, all the water tanks had been emptied and turned over during the night. She had assumed there would be plenty of water available at the start and had not saved enough of their own supply for their horses for the morning. Why on earth would the tanks have been dumped while there were still horses in camp? Maybe some poor volunteer had been a little too enthusiastic with their clean-up duties, but regardless, Flash and Brave were now unable to tank up before the start. Dehydration is one of the top reasons why horses fail metabolically during a ride, and Natalie was right to be concerned. Luckily, a well-prepared and generous soul offered them water from her own supply, and the Laws witnessed firsthand the generosity they would experience repeatedly along the trail in the coming hours.

It was time to ride!

Western States Trail Ride – Tevis Cup 100 Miles One Day – July 24, 2021

CHECKPOINT INFORMATION

Checkpoint	Mileage	From Robie	To Auburn	Check Type	Crew	Pulse	Cut-Off Times	Cut-Off Guidelines
Robie Park	0.0	0.0	100.0	Ride Start at: 5:15 am	Yes		5:30 am OUT	
Squaw High Camp	13.0	13.0	87.0	Water Only (Vet Available)	NO			7:45 am IN
Lyon Ridge	8.5	21.5	78.5	Trot-By (Vet Available)	NO			9:00 am IN
Red Star Ridge	7.0	28.5	71.5	Gate & Go ++	NO	60		10:00 am IN
Robinson Flat	7.5	36.0	64.0	Gate to Hold: 1 Hr.	Yes (1)	60	12:30 pm PULSE / 1:30 pm OUT	11:00 am IN
Dusty Corners	9.0	45.0	55.0	Water Only (No Check)	Ok (2)			
Last Chance	5.0	50.0	50.0	Gate & Go ++	NO	64	3:15 pm IN	3:00 pm IN
Devil's Thumb	4.0	54.0	46.0	Water only (No Check)	NO			4:30 pm IN
Deadwood	1.0	55.0	45.0	Gate & Go ++	NO	64	5:00 pm IN	
Michigan Bluff	7.5	62.5	37.5	Water Only (No Check)	Yes (3)			6:15 pm IN
Chicken Hawk	1.5	64.0	36.0	Gate and Go ++	Yes (4)	64		7:30 pm IN
Foresthill	4.0	68.0	32.0	Gate to Hold: 1 Hr.	Yes	64	8:45 pm PULSE / 9:45 pm OUT	8:00 pm IN
Cal 2	10.0	78.0	22.0	Hay & Water (No Check)	NO			11:45 pm IN
Francisco's	7.0	85.0	15.0	Gate & Go ++	NO	64	1:45 am IN	1:00 am IN
River Crossing	3.0	88.0	12.0	(No Check)	NO			
Lower Quarry	6.0	94.0	6.0	Gate & Go ++	NO	64	3:45 am IN / 4:00 am Out	3:30 am IN
No Hands Bridge	2.0	96.0	4.0	(No Check)	Ok (2)			
Auburn Staging Area	4.0	100.0	0.0	Timed Finish	Yes (5)		5:15 am	40 minutes to reach pulse at McCann
McCann Stadium	0.1	100.1		"Fit to Continue" Vet Release Examination (6)	Yes	64 / Sound		

"Gate" = when criteria reached, present horse. Criteria must be met within 30 min. of arrival+ After cut-off, Riders must leave 10 min. after vetting (1) Limit of one vehicle per rider with vehicle pass required and 2 crew members with wristband required. (2) Crews allowed, but not recommended. (3) Park short of Chicken Hawk Road and walk down to Michigan. (4) Walk in from Chicken Hawk Road. (5) Meet and walk with rider. (6) This mandatory vet exam, between 1 & 2 hours after McCann finish, does not affect finish status; vets want to assure themselves that all horses are okay. Haggin Cup exams are held on Sunday at 10:00 am–All First Ten Horses MUST remain at the Fairgrounds (See Rule 11) 6/4/2021

CHAPTER 13

No Turning Back

"It is not the mountain we conquer, but ourselves."
—SIR EDMUND HILLARY

They quietly made their way to Pen 2 and found a place to stand. They didn't want to be in the front of the Pen 2 starters, but they also didn't want to be stuck in the back where some of the more highly strung or inexperienced horses might be. They found themselves toward the front of the middle, right behind John, who had put Flash's hoof boots on the day before. Natalie had an unobstructed view over the heads of most people there since Brave was so tall, but Kyla was buried in a sea of restless bodies and found the experience a little disconcerting. Flash didn't seem too impressed either. Without much pomp and circumstance, they heard Pen 1 move out slowly. Then, from out of the darkness came a voice, "Pen 2 to the start line!"

As Pen 2 was released and the horses began gently surging forward into the darkness, Brave and Flash moved along with the crowd, taking their places in double, and then single, file as they left the graded dirt road and the Tevis trail began. As they got caught up in the bottleneck of the narrowing trail, Flash became agitated and Kyla had to work hard to keep him under control. It could be dangerous riding so close together at the start of a ride like this.

These horses were extremely fit and had spent a lot of time tied to their trailers and eating in the last forty-eight hours. There was a ton of pent-up energy vibrating through the horseflesh as they finally exploded onto the trail. The front runners had already disappeared, and Natalie and Kyla moved out with the group they found themselves in. They had little choice, anyway. It was like being carried along on a wave as it curled and rushed toward the shore. Everyone would feel better once the horses and riders spread out a little and the horses could settle down, each finding its own pace on the trail.

Kyla was glad to eventually get out of the crowd. But overexcitement at following the mass of horses streaming down the trail replaced Flash's frustration over the slow start. Kyla once again had to work to settle him down, and eventually they tucked in behind Brave and began moving along the trail at a nice trot.

Now that Flash had settled, Kyla got the chance to look around. To her surprise the sun had risen in the sky while she had been navigating Flash's antics. It was almost daylight. Kyla looked up at her mother and realized there was a definite benefit to being on a taller horse. Natalie was smiling and looking around at the beautiful morning, while Kyla was trying not to breathe too much of the trail dust into her lungs from the horses ahead of her.

Kyla also realized that she really needed to pee! She called to Natalie, who couldn't believe that they needed to stop this early in the race, just as they were finding their rhythm! Once all the riders spaced out a little, Natalie pulled Brave off to the side.

"Make it quick!" she told Kyla. "We need to keep moving."

One advantage to a short horse was the ease of getting off and on, and before long they were once again moving along the trail.

They made their way approximately five miles downhill to the Truckee River, and soon they could hear the early morning traffic making its way along Highway 89. The trail dropped below the road and continued beneath the overpass before emerging on the other side and winding sharply to the left where, for a brief instant, the riders found themselves along the side of the highway. There were volunteers up ahead who were ready to record the numbers of those riding by.

"Ninety-six," Natalie called out to them.

"Ninety-five J," Kyla called with her own number, the "J" indicating her junior rider status. All the horses had an identification number painted on their rumps with a wax marker to easily track them throughout the day. Those following the ride on the Tevis website could see their rider's number as it was recorded and follow their progress throughout the ride.

The volunteers smiled as they saw Kyla passing by on the proud little pony, his tail in the air and his expression all business.

"Cute pony!" one of them called out. Kyla smiled but felt like she may get tired of hearing that by the time the day was over.

After the highway crossing, they began winding up a series of steep switchbacks on part of a new trail that avoids parts of the original Tevis route now buried under the roads and civilization of Palisades Tahoe. The newer trail climbs upward, eventually becoming a wider road where overhead ski lifts sat out of season in the July heat. Had they been the skiers and snowboarders that carved these mountains every winter, their downward journey would have been far easier than what the Tevis competitors were asking their horses to do today.

The Laws watched how others paced their horses on the incline. They didn't want to burn their horses up by going too fast too early, but they also wanted to make time while the weather was cool. Flash maintained his quick little trot that he used to keep up with Brave's powerful walk. The horses' lungs expanded and collapsed like great bellows with every breath as their riders willed them to continue, onward and upward, one hoofbeat at a time. Natalie glanced back at Kyla occasionally, smiling as she saw her daughter reaching down to pat Flash on the neck, encouraging him to give his best effort.

Suddenly there was a commotion right behind them. A rider had come off her horse and was on the ground in a cloud of dust. Another rider had immediately grabbed the horse's bridle and already someone else had hopped off their horse to help the fallen rider from the ground and check for injuries. Concerned calls of "Are you okay?" rang out along the line of riders, each glad it wasn't their own horse that had slipped but knowing it could happen to them at any time.

Thankfully, all was well, and the rider remounted and continued onward, counting her blessings that her ride hadn't ended before the first official checkpoint. It was a reminder of the many opportunities for error and accidents along this journey, but Natalie and Kyla gathered up their reins and turned their focus again toward the slope ahead.

"Keep going," Kyla whispered to Flash. "You can do this!" And apparently Flash agreed. Without hesitation his little hooves began climbing again, head down, hind end working hard as he gained ground. It was a long climb with over 2,500 feet of elevation gain, but Kyla needn't have worried. Flash took on the steep trail with vigor and wild abandon. He never wavered. He chewed up the mountain, spat it out, and kept on chugging.

They hadn't gone far when Kyla pointed to a man standing at the side of the trail. He must have hiked all the way up in the dark earlier that morning to watch the competitors come through.

"Look at that man!" Kyla said. It wasn't just the fact he was there that caught her eye—he was also wearing a cape and a helmet with horns! He was standing there waving to each rider that passed, and his presence brought a smile to the faces of all those who were tackling the climb. The moment of levity gave everyone a chance to relax, drawing their tension away from the challenge they were undertaking and reminding them to take a deep breath and enjoy every moment of the experience itself.

The climb didn't end until they reached Watson's Monument, dedicated to the man who had rediscovered the emigrant trail that eventually became the Tevis Cup route. They had reached an elevation of 8,774 feet, the highest point of the historic trail. Unfortunately, it was far from being all downhill from there.

• • •

One of the most significant challenges of the Tevis Cup is its elevation changes that make most of the ride either relentless climbs or jaw-dropping descents. Occasional flatter sections allowed the horses to really move out and enjoy a moment's reprieve from the hill work, but these stretches were sparse. The ride had begun at an elevation of 7,200 feet, dropping 1,000 feet to the Highway 89 crossing. From there, they had now climbed another 1,700 feet to High Camp, where water tanks awaited the horses to rehydrate after their hard work.

At the water stop prior to reaching Watson's Monument, Natalie and Kyla had caught up to John again, and with all their horses drinking well they decided it was time to give them some electrolytes.

Electrolyte supplementation would help the horse replace all the salts and minerals they lost through sweating. An electrolyte depletion, which accumulates with distance, not only affects the horse's performance, but in rare instances it can become a medical emergency. Riders carried electrolytes in syringes in the packs usually attached to the horse's saddle. Unfortunately, John discovered that he had lost all the electrolytes he had been carrying on the trail; he must have left the zipper of his pack open, and they could be anywhere on the miles of trail behind them. They were now twelve miles into the ride, and the horses were working hard. Even though the temperatures were still cool they had all broken a sweat climbing the first mountain. Seeing John's dilemma, Natalie immediately dove into her own supply of electrolytes.

"After what you went through with Flash yesterday, the least I can do is share some of our electrolytes with you," she said, smiling, as she handed John enough to get him through to the next vet check.

While she knew that her own electrolyte stash had been carefully measured out for that section of trail, she also felt that if she did the right thing and shared what she had, everything would work itself out and she would be okay. This was one of those moments when her faith guided her, and besides, she had watched John wrestle tirelessly with Flash to put his boots on the day before. The man deserved a break.

Fresh in Natalie's mind were Kathie Perry's words from the ride meeting the day before: "Don't dilly dally at the stops. Those minutes add up. Do what you need to do and keep moving forward." So off they went again. It was another steep 1,000 feet of elevation gain before they would reach Watson's Monument and crest the mountain at Emigrant Pass. Kyla was more than impressed with her little pony. He had climbed that mountain fearlessly, and she hoped it was a sign of how he would tackle the rest of the day's challenges. It was still too early to tell how the miles would affect him as he trotted along. His legs took three times the number of steps that Brave did, but he was light on his feet, and thankfully Kyla was still light in the saddle.

As they reached the top, Natalie grabbed her phone to take pictures of what she was sure would be the most stunning vista she had ever seen, but a smokey haze covered everything. The distant fires obscured the views, instead offering vague shapes in the distance that teased of vistas beyond. Still, there was a sense of the vastness that this vantage point allowed—Squaw Peak to the south, Granite Chief to the north, Lake Tahoe back to the east, where they had come from. Nestled majestically amongst rugged mountain ranges of both California and Nevada, the lake was a magnet to those who could not resist the beauty of her shores. It was unfortunate that this year the smoke created a shadowy veil over all this natural beauty.

It was impossible to ride this part of the trail and not imagine the struggles those from a bygone era experienced as they navigated across the mountains to Auburn. Natalie and Kyla felt connected to those who had passed across the trail throughout history—the gold miners, the suppliers, the mules that had trudged along carrying gold pans, coffee, and canvas cloth to the new mining towns springing up everywhere as people envisioned a future rich in gold. Trappers had crossed these mountains hunting for pelts, had lived and died here. They would not have had the trail markers every half mile that today's travelers had, or vet checks where they could touch civilization for a moment to restock before continuing their journey. The trail had its own story, its own history, and Natalie and Kyla felt the privilege of being able to tread in the footsteps of those who had journeyed before them. The history was a palpable, living thing.

• • •

From here to Robinson Flat, the trail followed the historic Placer County Emigrant Road built in 1855. They continued on, winding around the mountain peak. Rocks clustered the side of the trail in wild abandon, and the hollow branches interrupted the green scrub covering the mountainside. The horses recovered quickly from the strain of the climb, their hooves tapping into a newfound energy as they trotted along, happy to be moving out at a fast clip once again. The Granite Chief Wilderness opened before them, the haze still softening the lines of the distant peaks and blending the trees into fuzzy shapes that dotted the mountainside. Natalie and Kyla looked around in awe. The red mountains of their home in Southern Utah were amazing, but this wilderness left them speechless.

The brief respite of easier footing soon gave way to the section of trail called "The Bogs," where mud and rocks teamed up to tear the boots off horses' hooves, and large boulders created a weaving and wonderful single track that enchanted before it struck with no mercy. Gray slabs of granite barely disguised as trail pulled the horses farther along, gradually leaving the higher peaks behind.

They were now dropping down to Lyon Ridge. After leaving the Granite Chief Wilderness, they found themselves straddling the high divide separating the watersheds of the Middle Fork and North Fork of the American River. This volcanic ridge repeatedly climbs and descends, and having a horse that could do more than a slow walk on the steep downhills came in handy. Flash was one of those horses who practically danced down the mountain, and to his credit, Brave did well keeping up with him. They were both good at placing their hooves to avoid rocks and potholes that dotted the trail, and by maintaining a good pace on the downhill as well as the uphill, Kyla and Natalie knew they were managing to stay ahead of the dreaded cutoff times at the vet checks. The horses drank well at Lyon Ridge, and it was now less than ten miles to their first vet check at Red Star Ridge, twenty-eight and a half miles into the ride. But first they had an important obstacle to traverse, the most photographed section of the Tevis Cup trail other than the finish itself: Cougar Rock.

• • •

Kyla had been particularly excited about the more technical parts of the trail, and most especially the famous Cougar Rock. Cougar Rock was a large piece of granite that rose like a monolith, offering riders a chance to get the most iconic photograph of their Tevis journey as their horses leapt and scrambled up its craggy surface. Taking on Cougar Rock was a risk. Every rider was offered the option to go around it, but few wanted to miss out on the experience of climbing it and getting the photograph so highly sought after. While most horses had no problem tackling Cougar Rock, there were stories—and videos—of horses slipping backward and riders dislodging from their saddles as horses bucked and staggered, trying to find their best footing on the granite's jagged surface. Sometimes there were impressive unplanned dismounts, and riders would then have to lead their horses to the top or grab their tails and have the horse pull them the rest of the way. It was extremely rare for a bad accident to occur with a horse falling or injuring itself, but it could happen. To document the Cougar Rock climb, a photographer perches above, out of the riders' path and ready to capture this dramatic moment while volunteers call words of encouragement and instruction to the horse and rider teams. One year, even the photographer fell off the rock.

As they approached this infamous landmark, Kyla insisted that her mother go first. Not because she was scared, but because she wanted to give Flash his head and go up at speed. She knew that with Brave ahead of them he would be more likely to go fast. She remembered a road trip their family had taken to Logan Canyon in Utah. When they were approaching a particularly steep section of road, her father had explained to her that in those circumstances you picked a path, put your foot on the gas, and used momentum to propel the vehicle forward and upward, not taking your foot off the gas until you crested the top. That was how Kyla planned on tackling Cougar Rock.

There was only one person ahead of the pair when they arrived. Kyla watched as the horse hesitated, then made the decision to go for it, scrambling quickly to the top. Once committed to his path, the horse and rider made easy work of it and had soon disappeared over its edge to continue their journey.

Now it was Natalie and Brave's turn. Brave was a very large and heavy horse. Although he was extremely fit and was used to technical trails, this section was particularly steep and difficult. At Natalie's urging he lived up to his name and surged forward. Halfway up the rock face, his front hoof slipped and he lost momentum. For a brief moment he came to a complete stop, hanging in limbo before somehow finding the strength to surge forward once again, launching his full weight off his hind legs and finally reaching flat land. They had done it!

Kyla watched from below, not fazed at all by what she had seen. "Come on, Flash! It's our turn! Let's go!" she said as she released her hold on Flash and he eagerly ran forward, completely undaunted by the jagged, gray granite monster looming ahead of him. He attacked the trail like it was put there purely for his own entertainment, hopping and skipping up the rock surface with Kyla smiling, laughing, and thoroughly enjoying the ride. He popped over the top, immediately looking around for Brave. Kyla could imagine him telling his friend, "That was fun! Can we do it again?" She gave him a quick pat on the neck before turning him down the trail once more. As much fun as that had been, they still had another six miles to go before arriving at Red Star Ridge.

It was warming up now. The sun was moving upward in the sky, and the warmth felt good after the cool morning temperatures. Both Natalie and Kyla understood that the sun pleasantly warming them now would relentlessly beat down on them and their horses later that day. There were still some hard climbs to do, but they easily made it through a section called Elephant's Trunk that scooped them along a short decline in the trail before a longer sweep uphill on loose rock and rubble as gray as the mammal this section was named after.

Finally, the trail opened up and followed Red Star Ridge, allowing the horses to once again find some relief, stretching out their hard-used muscles. Flash fell into an extended trot and easy canter while Brave gaited alongside him. They arrived at the Red Star Vet Check at 10:09 a.m., five hours after leaving Robie Park. It had been five hours of tough riding, and Natalie and Kyla were happy to let their horses drink and relax for a few moments. The horses were required to pulse down to 60 beats per minute before continuing, and the vets checked them thoroughly to make sure they were fit to continue. But there was no set hold time, and by 10:22 they were back on the trail, cruising westward along a wide gravel jeep road that would take them the remaining seven and a half miles to Robinson Flat.

The horses moved out eagerly, Brave giving Natalie a smooth ride as he found a nice, racking gait, while Flash trotted alongside his friend. Side by side their size difference was even more noticeable. Kyla had to crane her neck to look up at her mother who towered over her on the 16'3" hand Saddlebred. Now beside each other, Natalie took the chance to check in with Kyla, making sure she had been able to handle the morning's excitement so far.

"How does Flash feel, Kyla? He looks like he's doing well!"

"He's feeling good, just like he always has, so I don't think he's having a hard time carrying me so far."

"How are your knees?"

"They ache a little, but they're not too bad. I'll take something at Robinson Flat if I need to, but I think we're both doing okay right now. You and Brave look great, too, Mom!"

Kyla was feeling good. She had been slightly concerned about how Flash would be at the start of the ride. But besides being a bit of a handful at the very beginning, he had been giving Kyla his best effort, as if sensing that something about this ride was different and he needed to be on his best behavior. Kyla loved the feel of the little energetic pony beneath her. Her Pandora saddle was so comfortable, and she knew that they were done with the highest elevations. After Robinson Flat they would be dropping sharply down to under 2,000 feet. With the high country behind them, the smoke would be dissipating, and breathing would become easier. Kyla was looking forward to seeing her family as well as Shelah and Kacey at the vet check.

Kyla felt Flash stumble slightly, then continue on as if nothing had happened. But he didn't usually stumble, and she hoped that wasn't an indication of tiredness. Maybe she had spoken too soon when she said he seemed to be having no problem carrying her. Today would test Flash like no other race had, as well as Kyla. Kyla said a little prayer that they could pull whatever they needed from within themselves to reach the finish. Then she looked from her mother to the trail ahead and soldiered on.

CHAPTER 14

Robinson Flat

"Leave the road, take the trails."

—PYTHAGORAS

Coming into Robinson Flat seemed chaotic after the tranquility of the wilderness. It was a relief to see the familiar faces of their crew, and Natalie was once again happy that she had chosen people who fed her and Kyla's souls, as well as their bellies!

Kyla was hungry, which meant she was getting cranky. She hadn't been able to eat much before the start of the ride that morning, but after thirty-six miles she was ravenous and looking forward to a chance to eat and rest. She was thrilled that they had made it to the Robinson vet check and that they were an hour ahead of the dreaded cutoff time established by ride management. Many teams would be chasing that cutoff time all day and night, which added a lot of stress to an already challenging situation. Any delay or mishap could be the end of their ride.

As Kyla and Flash walked along the road, people began cheering and calling out encouragement to them both by name. It was a strange but wonderful feeling that all these strangers knew who they were and were rooting for them. The day was getting hotter. It was 11:30 and the sun was high in the sky as riders jostled for space and the elusive slivers of shade thrown down from the trees along the side of the road.

"Natalie! Kyla! Over here!" The familiar sound of Shelah's voice had never sounded so good! They saw Kacey bringing the collapsible cart toward them, and in what seemed like a split second the saddles were pulled and the bridles removed. There was Adam and James. Seeing them made the morning feel longer than it had been. The faces of the crew were such a welcome sight, but there was no time to give in to emotion; they needed to get through the vet check.

Crews swarmed across the landscape, resembling busy worker ants each focused on their tasks, descending hungrily on their horse and rider team as they made the approach. In addition to crews, volunteers, vets and their scribes, photographers, and ride management all thronged together, busy with their specific task. This year was a little more chaotic than usual as crews squeezed their teams into the limited space along the road and vets were displaced to the area by the main entrance road. But Team Law didn't know anything different since this was their first time at the vet check.

Adam had stopped to pick up Starbucks sandwiches on the way in, and even though both girls were starving they knew they needed to take the horses to see the vets before they could rest and take time to eat. Satisfied that both horses looked good, they headed toward the vet check area, offering them water from the large tubs along the way. Both horses drank well and seemed bright eyed, not in the least bothered by the difficult thirty-six miles they had traveled so far. As the diminutive Flash trotted eagerly up to the line of vets, he carried himself confidently, as if he had no doubt he had every right to be there competing against the fittest Arabian horses in the world. Smiles broke out on dust-covered faces as he passed by.

"How's he doing so far?" the vet asked Kyla as he held the stethoscope against Flash's girth area.

"He's amazing!" Kyla beamed. "He flew up Cougar Rock like it was nothing!"

"I can imagine!" the vet said, smiling at the thought. "Okay, trot him out to the cone and back. You know what to do."

Kyla complied and when Flash returned the vet nodded and finished his examination. He listened to Flash's heart rate once again, then noted, "His CRI is 60/56 and he looks great. He's lost a boot, though. He's still sound, but keep an eye on that."

Flash was deemed fit to continue, receiving all A's on his vet card, apart from a couple of B's on gut sounds. Natalie and Kyla decided to leave things as they were regarding the boot. There wasn't anyone around to help them glue on another one, and if one had come off already, the chances were high that he would lose more. Kyla wondered if he had lost it when she felt him stumble and hoped it had been from the boot and not from tiredness like she had assumed. According to the vet he was doing well, and Kyla felt relieved that they would be able to continue after their hold time was up.

Kyla pulled Flash off to one side to watch her mom vet through with Brave, who had been patiently waiting his turn. While Brave pulsed down to fifty-six beats per minute on his first heart rate check, Natalie then made the mistake of feeding him a handful of hay before his CRI was completed, forgetting that he still had to have his heart rate checked again after the trot out. When the vet took his heart rate a second time, the number was elevated to sixty-four, and even though the vet suspected it may have been from the hay there was no way to be sure.

"I'm sorry, but you'll have to bring him back for a recheck before you leave," he told Natalie. "I think he's fine, but as well as an inverted CRI his gut sounds are a C, and I want to make sure they improve after he has a chance to eat. Come back in thirty minutes."

At first, Natalie wasn't overly worried. She had ridden her horse thousands of miles, and she could read him well. His attitude was good, he had felt strong on the trail, and it was not unusual for some horses to have low gut sounds at this point in a ride. If this had been a fifty-mile ride with only fourteen miles to go, Natalie would have been confident that he would finish strong. But this was the Tevis Cup, and although the higher elevations of the first thirty-six miles had been challenging, the steep canyons of the next section would plunge horse and rider into the sticky heat trapped in their depths. The vet would not send a horse back out onto the trail if there was any indication that he could have a serious issue before the next checkpoint. The crew would need to pay extra attention to getting Brave hydrated and eating well to get his gut sounds moving, or they could be in trouble. Doubt crept in and Natalie could not help but feel stressed as a little voice in her head ran through the what-ifs. What if they had gone a little too fast on the good footing? What if he wasn't ready for a race of this caliber? What if he were pulled, as so many horses are at Robinson? It would be the end of the Tevis journey not only for her but also for Kyla and Flash, who wouldn't be allowed to continue alone.

"I'm sure Brave will be fine," she reassured Kyla even though she wasn't sure herself. But there was nothing much she could do about the past, so they made their way back to where the crew had set everything up, determined to help Brave recover as best they could.

Shelah gave both horses their dry mash of Outlast. It would have been better for Brave to have eaten a wet mash, but he wasn't used to it and Shelah felt it would be good to get the high density Outlast into his stomach and then work on the hydration issue separately. Both horses ate their entire pan, and Flash also managed to find some leftover mash another horse had abandoned and ate that as well. Shelah offered them both hay and was pleased at how well they both ate throughout the one-hour hold time. It was hard for Natalie to stop obsessing over the horses and relax, but her crew insisted that she let go of her responsibilities for just a few minutes to recharge for the tough leg of the journey ahead.

James and Adam followed Shelah's orders. They had never crewed before and had no idea what they were supposed to do, but just their presence brought a sense of comfort to their family and a sense of normalcy to a crazy situation. They made sure that both Natalie and Kyla ate and drank well, and then Adam refilled their water bottles and CamelBak hydration systems, dissolving the Hammer electrolyte tablets that came with their rider packets inside. The tablets had a pleasant taste, which they found easier to stomach than the plain water they were constantly drinking. Kyla enjoyed the grape flavor, and Natalie made a mental note to order some for future rides. Kyla also drank a Coke and ate sour jelly beans, salt and vinegar chips, and Doritos. Natalie hoped that Kyla's young body would let her know when she needed something more substantial to eat, but at least she was eating something.

"How's it been going, Kyla?" Kacey asked as Kyla crunched through her bag of chips. "How did it feel going over Cougar Rock?"

Natalie watched the girls chat, filled with happiness that Kacey had agreed to come along and help them. It was good for Kyla to have someone close to her own age to help her decompress at the vet checks and encourage her with all that was ahead. Kyla would need Kacey more and more as the day unfolded.

After thirty minutes they took Brave back to the vet, where he trotted out for his CRI recheck, which showed a score of 52/56. The improvement, and his improved gut sounds, made the vets confident that Brave was sufficiently recovered to continue. What a relief! All the extra time with the vet meant they now had to rush to re-tack the horses to leave on time. They made sure to give both horses a good dose of electrolytes and then headed over to the out-timer's station to be cleared to leave.

On their way, they ran into Cassee Steed Terry, a friend who had vetted some endurance rides. She was there crewing for another team, and she reminded them that the upcoming canyons would be hot. "Douse your shirts now," she advised them, "and at any opportunity you get during this leg of the race to help combat the heat." Cassee's reminder reinforced Natalie's awareness that she needed to be on top of her game and remember strategies like these to help not only herself but also her thirteen-year-old daughter get safely through the long hours ahead.

As they passed the out-timers table, they were asked for the slips they received with the times they had entered the vet check and the time the horses had pulsed down. Another moment of panic ensued as Natalie realized they had left them back at their camp out during the check. Luckily Kacey was young and fast and she ran back to get them.

There seemed to be a million little things to remember and do at each stop. It was amazing how this ride seemed to have more details to stay on top of than the other rides the pair had done. Rider and crew needed to be well prepared at Tevis, where even a small mistake could cause a problem later. They felt the added weight of competing in the Tevis Cup once again as they headed off on one of the most grueling parts of the ride. The Canyons.

CHAPTER 15

The Canyons

*"As human beings, we have the innate need
to explore, to see what is around the corner."*

—JIMMY CHIN

As the mother and daughter team left Robinson Flat, they found
themselves riding alone. They were both relieved they hadn't been
one of the many teams to be pulled at Robinson and were glad for
the one-hour cushion they had when arriving at the vet check to
help absorb the extra ten minutes they had taken before heading
back out on the trail. Natalie had heard the next thirty-two miles
to Foresthill were challenging and had been forewarned about the
heat of the canyons and the steep switchback trails they would be
descending. Many riders hiked into the canyons to take the weight
off their horses' backs and, if physically fit enough, they "tailed" up
the steep trails—holding onto their horses' tails and being pulled up
the trail on foot.

There was a nice wide forest road heading out of Robinson Flat—a
former wagon route used in the late 1800s—and the horses eagerly
picked up their pace. The trail passed over a summit and traversed
Cavanaugh Ridge, where Natalie and Kyla noted that the smoke
seemed to be easing off. Maybe the wind had shifted direction again.
The ridgeline trail was full of loose and embedded rocks, and Kyla could
feel the rocks bouncing off Flash's hooves. They were slowly losing elevation, the muggy, sweltering depths of the canyons approaching fast.

They reached Dusty Corners, where the horses drank well before the short stretch to the next vet check at Last Chance, a now abandoned town that perches precariously on the edge of a promontory overlooking the American River.

There was no hold time at Last Chance. It was, quite literally, the last chance for the vets to check each horse once more before they plunged into the canyon abyss. It was critical that a horse not doing well at this point be pulled from the ride, as there was no way to get a trailer into the canyons to rescue a horse in trouble. Horses and riders were required to get in and out under their own steam. Natalie was thrilled to see that Brave had significantly better vet scores at this check than the last one. He received mostly A's with only a couple of B's, and his heart rate was at 52. With Brave's scores, Natalie felt even more confident in tackling the trail ahead.

This time it was Flash who was showing some issues they would need to watch. His gut sounds on two of the four quadrants were a C, and he needed to hydrate more. The vet even noted on his vet card that he looked tired. This was a first for the little pony who never seemed to show any signs of exhaustion. Now it was Kyla's turn to worry.

"I'm too big for him, Mom! I'm asking too much of him," she said as they watered the horses once more.

"I think the vets are just being cautious," Natalie reassured her. "He'll be okay. A lot of athletes have a dip in their energy at some point during a race. Once we get down to the river, we'll take a few extra minutes to cool him off. If you're really worried, maybe lay off the goldfish crackers for a while!" Seeing the look on her daughter's face, she added, "I'm kidding, Kyla! Eat as much as you want. You hardly weigh a thing! Flash will be fine, I promise!"

The narrow trail leading from Last Chance drops 2,000 feet that seem never ending. Natalie had considered getting off and hiking down to the river crossing, but when she got to that part in the trail, she realized that Brave could probably navigate it just as well with her on his back. For Brave and Flash, even the steep switchbacks heading into the first canyon were easier than some of the trails they often traveled back home, and they passed other riders as they made their way toward the river crossing and the famous swinging bridge. Despite the concerns at the vet check, Flash was acting fine, and Kyla could tell he was enjoying every moment. There was nothing too steep, too technical, or with too much of a drop off to faze him. As Kyla's confidence in his ability to carry her returned, she gave Flash his head and allowed him to do what he did best. He popped down the steep and dusty trail, flowing around the tight corners of the switchbacks, his legs and feet moving forever downward in a controlled but constant descent.

As they made the final switchback, the sound and smell of the river engulfed their senses. They were thankful to have finally reached this place where they could take a few minutes to rest. As Brave approached the river, his back hooves slipped on some slick granite and he slid a few feet, managing to catch himself before he would have plunged into the bushes up ahead. Natalie caught her breath, hoping the unplanned slide had not caused an injury. To avoid the same thing happening, Kyla picked her way around the granite slab so Flash could avoid the slick surface.

Brave appeared fine, but Natalie was grateful for the river's cool water to soak his legs, just in case there had been any damage to them she couldn't see. She needed to be on constant lookout for the safest route possible. This wasn't like at home where it was fun to challenge the horses with technical trails. The temperature, smoke, and long miles dotted with rocks and boulders made this trail hard enough on its own without looking for any additional thrills.

The river was magical, and there was another rider on a beautiful Kiger mustang standing in the water and enjoying the moment. It felt as if they had entered a painting. Everything was more vibrant than it could possibly be in real life. Brave and Flash plunged willingly into the welcome coolness, and as Brave went in up to his knees, Kyla hopped off Flash and walked in with him.

"Look at all the fish!" she exclaimed as rainbow trout darted through the clear, dappled water to move out of their way. The river wasn't as cold as she had expected, and Flash went in over his belly and would have gone for a swim if Kyla hadn't been holding his reins. The water was refreshing, and although they remembered Kathie Perry's reminder to "Never hurry, never tarry," they decided that this would be the one spot where it would be okay to ignore that advice and savor the healing powers of the mountain water, especially with the long climb out of the canyon ahead. Besides, Lindsay Fisher, who Natalie had met at the City of Rocks ride and whose horse Monk had won the Haggin Cup the previous Tevis, had reminded Natalie to not let the horses start the climb out of the canyon until they had completely cooled off. The minutes they lost in the water would be more than made up by having strong horses in the miles ahead.

Feeling good after the experience at the river, they both mounted and made their way up the bank to the swinging bridge entrance. The bridge was only about three feet wide, just wide enough for a horse to fit through comfortably. It was sixty feet long and appeared quite sturdy. It had been rebuilt in 2014 after the American Fire had destroyed the original bridge. But it wasn't called the swinging bridge for nothing.

Brave was unsure about this strange obstacle and refused to step onto it, but Flash happily took the lead and calmly walked over as if he crossed a swinging bridge every day. Kyla held her breath as she crossed, the strange feeling of the bridge moving beneath Flash's hooves making her a little anxious. It felt as if Flash were walking on a tightrope. Luckily, it didn't take long to cross, and once Brave saw his friend crossing the bridge with no issues, he followed happily behind. It was to become a common pattern on the rest of the ride: when Brave was hesitant about a situation, he would rely on his tiny emotional support pony to show him that all was well!

The next challenge was climbing 1,600 feet of elevation out of the canyon toward Devil's Thumb—a fifty-foot volcanic outcropping that jutted from the forest against the horizon. The climb was an endless series of well graded switchbacks that gave no reprieve to those scrambling out of the depths of the canyon. The Laws stayed on for the climb, but if the horses had shown signs of stress they would have dismounted and walked beside or behind them. Although the climb seemed to go on forever, the horses put their heads down and plugged away, putting one hoof in front of the other and gradually gaining ground. The climb up to Devil's Thumb reminded Natalie and Kyla of a trail behind their house in Utah that took them from 3,500 feet of elevation to 10,000 feet. It was nearly identical except for the foliage. Brave and Flash both knew how to put themselves into four-wheel drive and power up. They didn't rush, they didn't push, they just climbed.

Once they could see the volcanic outcropping of Devil's Thumb, they knew that the climb was almost over. The horses were happy to have a long, refreshing drink before the short ride into the Deadwood vet check. Crews didn't come into Deadwood, but Tevis Cup volunteers did, and Natalie and Kyla were so grateful they made the effort, bringing watermelon and cantaloupe, as well as cold drinks for the riders. It was amazing to think that it took around eight hundred volunteers every year to pull off an event like the Tevis Cup. That year, these numbers worked out to seven volunteers per horse and rider team!

When the horses were presented to the vets at Deadwood, Flash showed improved scores on his vet card with almost all A's. Brave had B's on his gut sounds but otherwise had all A's as well. Natalie and Kyla were glad they had given the horses time to relax in the river. It had cooled them down and refreshed them mentally for the ride ahead.

The girls now had a thirteen-mile trek to the next one-hour hold at Foresthill. The trail led past the cemetery at Deadwood and then descended 2,500 feet over the next three miles to the bottom of yet another canyon. El Dorado Canyon was a deep gulch that sucked all the hot air in the vicinity into it, causing the horses and riders to struggle through stifling temperatures on the myriad treacherous switchbacks before reaching the canyon floor. The combination of bare rock and lack of shade trees made the canyon ten to twenty degrees hotter than other parts of the trail. With every downward step that Flash took, Kyla was thinking about the same number of steps he would have to take upward again. It was beginning to feel torturous. But no one had ever said that Tevis was easy.

The trail out of El Dorado Canyon was, indeed, steep, with precarious drop-offs and views that opened up and distracted the weary riders from slogging out of her depths. Once again, they kept a steady pace, moving onward, always having forward motion, never taking any long stops, and they were rewarded at the end of El Dorado Canyon when they emerged from the trail to find themselves in the small town of Michigan Bluff.

• • •

Michigan Bluff was Natalie's favorite stop of the whole Tevis experience. The town was adorable, its character-filled mountain homes perched on the edge of the American River gorge. It seemed as if the whole town came out to help the riders passing through. This was a difficult place for crews to access due to limited parking, and since Foresthill was just a few miles ahead most crews chose to wait there for their riders. There used to be a vet check at Michigan Bluff, but now the vet check was at Chicken Hawk, just a mile or so along the trail.

But even so, volunteers and locals filled the streets of Michigan Bluff, offering hay, water, and encouragement to the teams coming through. Since the Tevis Cup had been passing through this way for well over half a century, the locals knew what to do and were happy to do it. They gladly offered their garden hoses to fill the water tubs and shouted words of encouragement to the teams who had just tackled the infamous canyons, lifting their spirits for the short trek to Foresthill.

As usual, Flash garnered all the attention as they cooled their horses and grabbed some of the refreshing fruit offered to them by the wonderful volunteers. The watermelon washed the dust out of their throats and helped to quench their thirst. Kyla, realizing how close they were to the next one-hour hold, was eager to move along. Her clothes were sweaty and damp, and she was feeling the effects of the canyons and the late afternoon heat. It was beginning to feel like a *really* long day.

Natalie and Kyla arrived at Chicken Hawk at 6:44 p.m. The vet check there was only four miles from the vet check and one-hour hold at Foresthill, but the vets wanted to make sure that all the horses who had suffered through the canyons were still fit to continue. Natalie and Kyla had been in the saddle for almost fourteen hours. The horses had traversed sixty-four miles of trail and the high country, and formidable canyons were now behind them. The sun was dropping ever lower in the sky, and the areas thick with fir and pine were even darker in the shadows of dusk.

Kyla knew they would be traversing the remaining thirty-six miles in total darkness, with only the light from the Tevis moon and some strategically placed glow bars to guide them along the trails. She could feel her anxiety growing, and what had seemed like a fun adventure in the light of day was fast becoming her biggest nightmare. The fact that Flash had once again received mostly A's on his vet card didn't assuage her fears of what was up ahead. Brave came through the vet check with a mixture of A's and B's on his card, and a C on one of his gut quadrants. Natalie was relieved. For a large horse who had just gone through two major canyons, Brave was doing amazingly well. She was more concerned about Kyla, who had become noticeably quiet, internalizing her anxiety over what was ahead. Natalie looked forward to Foresthill, where they would have their spirits buoyed by their crew, and could rest, eat, and prepare for the final thirty-two-mile push to the finish.

• • •

To add insult to injury, the Western States Trail throws in an extra canyon between Michigan Bluff and Foresthill—Volcano Creek Canyon. The two-mile descent into a boulder strewn creek crossing then takes the riders on a mile-and-a-half ascent to the western boundary of Tahoe National Forest, where they emerge from the dusty trail onto Bath Road. Bath Road winds upward for about half a mile and is often scattered with a few diligent crew members who feel the urge to hike down and meet their rider with cool water to douse the horses and words of encouragement that the vet check is just up ahead.

Signs of civilization appeared the closer they got to the vet check, but Natalie and Kyla were unsure how soon they should dismount to allow the horses' heart rates to drop before coming into the pulse check area. Previous knowledge and experience of either riding or crewing Tevis would have been valuable here, as Bath Road is longer than most first-time riders realize. At the approach to the vet check, people line the road cheering and clapping as they watch teams emerge from this tough leg of the race. There are huge tubs of fresh water for the horses with hoses that run from the back of locals' homes. Just like in Michigan Bluff, these residents have become a part of the Tevis experience over the years, looking forward to the procession of horses and riders briefly taking over their world.

Natalie and Kyla had no idea they should have waited to get closer to this busy checkpoint and jumped off their horses far too early, even stripping tack before their crews could reach them. Natalie knew there was a problem with one of Flash's boots. It had been flopping and folding under his hoof as he moved, but there was too much glue remaining to pull it off. Natalie knew that it was important to get the boot off as soon as possible once they reached the vet check. She had called ahead to Shelah with her concerns, and Shelah had the hoof armor ready and on standby to apply once the boot had been removed. Both right boots had now been lost on the trail since that morning, and one of the left ones was failing. They would need to decide quickly whether to leave the one remaining boot on his front left hoof or have it pulled while they were at Foresthill, where a farrier would be on standby.

Once Natalie texted Shelah they were in, the crew jumped into high gear, getting themselves and the crew-cart farther down the road to meet their riders so they could begin cooling to encourage their heart rates to drop.

"Kyla! Kyla! How's Flash doing?" a woman sitting in a camp chair by the side of the road called out.

"Looking good, Kyla. Go, Flash!" called another.

Kyla was again surprised when she heard onlookers calling her and Flash by name. It was strange, but it was also nice to hear support and encouragement from total strangers. As she listened, she began to hear murmurings from the crowd that Flash looked a little lame as he walked up the road. Kyla had noticed that his gait had changed on the downhill portion of Volcano Canyon, and now she was concerned that he may be sore in the shoulder from all the steep downhills. Or maybe, with the loss of two boots on the right side, he could have been traveling unbalanced for several miles. If he didn't pass this vet check, their journey would be over, and Natalie would have to finish the ride alone.

Natalie and Kyla were also feeling the effects of straddling a horse for sixty-eight miles in clothes that had become dirty and sweaty. Chafing was a problem that could take a rider out of a race. Wet skin and constant friction was a recipe for disaster, and if the girls didn't get that situation sorted out as soon as possible, they may not be able to mount up for the final part of the race.

The stress of unknowns with Flash and the darkness she would have to ride through up ahead weighed heavily on Kyla, and Shelah noticed the difference in the girl immediately. Kyla was feeling tired for the first time that day, and the fear of riding in the dark was creeping into her bones and taking hold. The shadows of the trees lining Bath Road stretched and lengthened as the sun went down in the sky, and Kyla shuddered as the darkness engulfed them, knowing that this was where her Tevis challenge truly began.

CHAPTER 16
Foresthill

"Have faith in the journey. Everything had to happen exactly as it did to get you where you're going next."

—MANDY HALE

Shelah and Kacey had been waiting for their riders at Foresthill for quite some time. They had managed to take an hour and a half nap in between the vet checks but spent the rest of the time driving, running errands, and organizing what the riders and horses would need at this vitally important checkpoint. After this, the riders would be plunged into the darkness on some very precarious trails, and the crew needed to make sure they did everything possible to prepare them for the miles ahead, knowing that after sixty-eight miles of riding they would all be feeling depleted and sore.

Crews have their own kind of endurance event. They run around nonstop, and when they finally feel they have everything done, they sit down to worry about their team, wondering where they are and how they're doing and hoping they don't find out they've been pulled since the last vet check. Kacey was amazed at how Shelah was holding it together despite being sick. She was on top of every situation and gave clear, concise instructions whenever there was something to be done. The woman was a born leader.

Shelah was equally impressed with Kacey, whose maturity went far beyond her teenage years. She followed direction well, never whined or complained, and offered both Kyla and Natalie emotional support at every opportunity. Both Shelah and Kacey also made sure to feed and take care of themselves. They had already been crewing for fourteen hours, but they would need to be there for their teams until the end of the ride and beyond. The horses would need care and supervision after the finish, and part of the crew duties was to provide this and let the riders get some sleep.

Having finally received the call their riders were in, Shelah and Kacey jumped into action. They hosed off the horses, and with Kacey dragging the cart filled with the discarded tack the final hundred yards up the road, they all made a sharp left into the open area of the vet check.

Shelah immediately turned to Kyla. "Why don't you leave Flash with me and Kacey and go straight to the trailer? You need to find the chafing cream and get some food into you. Hopefully there will be time for you to rest here for a little bit and take a nap."

"What about his boot and the vet check?" Kyla asked her, concerned that it was more than just a loose shoe causing his uneven gait.

"We can handle that. I'll send Kacey back to find you if there's anything wrong, okay? Just go and relax!"

This last request was more like a command, but Kyla was more than happy to comply. With one last look at Flash and knowing he was in excellent hands, she left to find the trailer with all their supplies. As she walked to the horse trailer, she noticed that rigs clustered the outer rim of the vetting area, having made their way down from Robie Park earlier that day. Some had left once their riders had made it through the checkpoint, but many were still parked there. It looked like all the other ride camps that Kyla had been to, except there were vendors selling food and drinks, and at least a dozen porta potties were lined up against a bank of trees in the center of the field. The vet check was at the site of an old sawmill, so there was plenty of space to spread out and take advantage of the last piece of civilization they would encounter until the finish in Auburn.

Kyla had reached the truck and trailer only to find it was locked so she couldn't access any of their supplies. She was about to walk over to the vetting area to get the keys when her eyes fell on a blackberry bush poking out of the foliage behind the trailer. She happily began shoveling as many as she could gather into her mouth, amazed that her favorite fruit was magically put right in front of her like a gift from the heavens! So long as she had berries, she was happy to wait until someone came back to the trailer with the keys. There was nothing inside the trailer that she would prefer to eat anyway.

Meanwhile, Natalie and the crew walked the horses over to the pulse takers, who deemed that both were below the criteria and could vet in at any time. Strangely, the only secure boot remaining on Flash was the one that John had the hardest time putting on. With only one and a half boots in place and both on his left side, it made sense to have the farrier remove all the boots so Flash would be even on all four feet, and hopefully comfortable. Since the line to vet in the horses was short, they decided to vet the horses through before seeing the farrier, and Shelah snapped the offending half-off boot back into place as they fell into line for the final one-hour vet check of the ride. Shelah and Kacey trotted both horses out for the vet with Flash showing off as usual. The further they got into the ride, the more impressed the vets and spectators became as they watched Flash trot out with great impulsion and eagerness. There was no doubt that he enjoyed these moments of being the center of attention, and the people loved him. His fan club was growing larger by the minute. Kacey had been posting updates to his Facebook page, and his number of followers was growing the farther Flash went along the trail.

At mile sixty-eight Flash got mostly A's on his vet card with a few B's, but his CRI was a perfect 52/52! Natalie was amazed at how well Brave was handling the trail as well. His heart rate was coming down below criteria with no problems. His vet scores were a little lower than Flash's, but he got a perfect CRI of 56/56. Happily, both horses were cleared to continue, and now it was time to take care of the boot issue once and for all.

Separating the horses at this point would not have been a good idea. They would have fussed, and it would have been harder for Joby, the farrier, to work on Flash. The crew brought feed and water to both horses while Flash was being worked on so they wouldn't have to miss out on time to eat during the hold. When the farrier asked Natalie what to put on Flash's hooves instead, both Natalie and Shelah replied "nothing" in unison. They knew that Flash's hooves were tough and hoped he would be fine for the remaining miles. Joby looked at them with concern but did as they asked. Shelah applied the hoof armor to all four hooves, and she and Natalie led the horses back to the trailer, Kacey dragging all their supplies in the cart behind them.

Now it was a rush to get everything done at the vet-check due to the extra time it had taken dealing with the boot issue. Natalie and Kyla immediately went to change their clothing while the crew saw to the horses and made sure they had more mash and as much hay as they could snack on. As Shelah was brushing the dirt and sweat from Brave's back she noticed that he was flinching every time she brushed a certain area.

"Natalie, come look at this," Shelah called, not wanting to concern her friend but knowing she needed to be aware of the situation.

"Look how he's flinching away from me when I brush his back just behind the saddle. I think it's too far back for the saddle pad to be rubbing, but I want to put a fresh pad on him just in case."

"Good idea" Natalie replied. Then a thought dawned on her. "I think that might be where the water scoop was hitting him," she told Shelah. She had attached a scoop to Brave's saddle so she could cool him off by pouring water on his neck and inner legs at any water sources that allowed it. The scoop could have been knocking against that place on his back as he was trotting and may well have made him sore over the long distance they had traveled. Now it was evening, and it was unlikely she would need the scoop anymore anyway.

"Let's cover our bases and remove the scoop and change the saddle pad as well," Natalie decided. "Good catch, Shelah."

James had picked up some fried chicken for the girls to eat, and by this time they were ravenous and tucked into it with great enthusiasm. Natalie had memories of eating fried chicken whenever she and her father had gone deep sea fishing, so not only did the food fill her belly, but it also offered her emotional comfort. It was exactly what she needed at this point in the ride. The day was wearing on her, and she was struggling not to show it. She knew that Kyla was battling her own demons with the ensuing darkness, and Natalie was determined to remain as positive and supportive as she could for her daughter in the miles ahead. The cots were still set up in the back of the horse trailer, and with only fifteen minutes left to go before their out-time, Natalie and Kyla laid down together for a quick eight-minute power nap. She wrapped her arms around her daughter and held her close, comforting her and letting her know that she would never be alone. Not on this ride, not in the days afterwards, and not for the rest of her life.

• • •

The nap was far too brief. They would have preferred eight hours, but eight minutes would have to do. While they were resting, Shelah and Kacey saw to the needs of the horses, gave them their electrolytes, and got the tack ready for the night section of the ride. For a novice Tevis crew, they were doing an amazing job. The sky was getting darker with each second, and the full moon was rising as the crew checked the string of fairy lights that Natalie had put on Brave's breast collar the previous day. All they had to do was turn them on before they left. Since Flash didn't wear a breast collar, Natalie had made a necklace out of fairy lights for him. She had carefully researched the effect light had on a horse's ability to see at night and had discovered that red lights were easiest on the horse's eyes. Although the fairy lights would not help them see the trail, it would help them see each other and for others to see them as they rode through the town of Foresthill. The team would most likely turn the lights off once they got onto the main section of trail and let the horses use their natural night vision to navigate the California Street Trail that would take them all the way down to the American River once again.

There would be no room for error on this part of the trail; the drop offs plunged hundreds of feet and could result in severe injury and even death to a horse and rider should they fall. They had all heard the stories over the years of an occasional horse that had slipped off the trail and needed to be rescued. It was extremely rare for a fatality to happen, but the ride organizers had emergency plans in place and were ready to leap into action at a moment's notice if necessary. Foresthill was at an elevation of 3,225 feet, and they would be descending to around 700 feet to reach Francisco's and Lower Quarry checkpoints. This was the last downhill section of the ride, and there would be multiple checkpoints in the final miles of the course as the distance and hours on the trail tested everyone's endurance. As well as being afraid of riding this section in the dark, Natalie knew that Kyla was concerned with mountain lions and bears that may be out on the trail, lurking in the shadows. Natalie tried to reassure her that it was unlikely that anything would disturb the riders making their way along the trail, but just the thought they were out there *somewhere* added to Kyla's overall sense of unease.

Once the horses were tacked up, Natalie and Kyla emerged from the trailer in their fresh riding outfits and with a renewed sense of determination to finish what they had started. Even though Kyla was extremely worried, there wasn't any consideration of quitting. Natalie had been raised to set goals and not stop until she had achieved them, and she had raised her daughter the same way.

Before leaving Foresthill, Adam held his daughter close and reminded her to have faith in what she was doing. He pointed out that although she would be facing her fears in the coming darkness, her faith would always be there as a beacon of light. He would be waiting for them both at the finish line and praying for their safe arrival. And with that thought, Kyla put her foot in the stirrup, mounted, and got ready to follow her mother through whatever was ahead.

• • •

Even though her stirrup lengths hadn't changed since she had last dismounted Flash, once Kyla mounted him again, they just didn't feel right to her. She commented to her mother that they felt too short and something was wrong. Knowing they hadn't been changed, Natalie told her she didn't want to waste any more time and they needed to get going. They had left Robinson ten minutes late, and she didn't want to lose any more precious minutes when every second could mean the difference between completing or being pulled at one of the upcoming vet checks for missing a cutoff time.

The grit and determination that drove Natalie at this point of the ride would aid them in finishing their goal, but it also took her mind momentarily off the needs of her daughter—something she had just sworn to herself would be her main priority. Shelah heard the exchange and immediately moved to Kyla's side to lower the stirrups. It was important that Kyla felt as comfortable as possible, and looking back, Natalie appreciated that this was what a great crew did. They stepped in and made decisions when the riders were too trail weary to make the right ones themselves. Once Kyla was comfortable, Natalie smiled at Shelah, whispered a silent thank you, and they left the vet check just three minutes past their designated out-time.

The air was cool as they made their way out of the dirt driveway and onto the trail that ran alongside Foresthill Road heading toward the town, ready to tackle whatever was up ahead.

Riding through the town of Foresthill in the dark, with their fairy lights dancing in sync with their horses' movements, was one of Kyla's favorite memories. Foresthill was a true mountain town, with small retail businesses and restaurants lining the main street. The town came alive for the Tevis event, and there was a sense of camaraderie among the people sitting on their truck beds or pouring out of the buildings as the horses passed by. Kyla could hear the exclamations of "Oh, look! It's a little pony!" And, of course, Flash put on his usual show for his admirers whom he assumed had gathered only for him as he made his way along the street. Kyla smiled as she felt him puff out his chest and pick his feet up just a little higher, but she also knew this would be the last sign of civilization for a while. She inhaled the familiar comfort of it, knowing that soon they would be sucked into the darkness and desolation of the trail ahead.

They took a left turn off the main street toward the entrance of the trail and found themselves behind two riders, each on a gray horse with glow sticks strapped to their breast collars. They watched in horror as one of the horses suddenly slipped and fell to its knees onto the rough surface. The rider was unharmed and immediately jumped off the horse, checking to make sure that it hadn't sustained any injuries. Luckily, the horse seemed fine, and the rider remounted and continued along the trail. But seeing this happen right in front of her rattled Kyla's nerves even more. At thirteen, Kyla wasn't even sure that she belonged on this ride that was becoming harder and harder by the hour. Her youth, the fact that Flash was so small, and her insecurities about her physical and mental ability to finish the race crowded in and took hold. She breathed deeply and tried to remember the feeling of her dad's arms around her and his words about faith.

Neither Kyla nor Natalie was aware that 54 out of 133 competitors had already been pulled from the race, and just the fact that they were still there, heading out for the last thirty-two miles, was an amazing accomplishment already.

CHAPTER 17

Into the Darkness

"Everything you've ever wanted is on the other side of fear."

—GEORGE ADDAIR

Before heading down the steepest part of the California Street Trail, Natalie was incredibly pleased to see that the two horses that had just caught up to them were none other than the famous Monk, usually ridden by Lindsay Fisher but this year piloted by her friend Nancy Martin, and Lindsey herself riding another of her horses, Bucephalos, who happened to be Monk's sire. Natalie and Lindsay had met at the City of Rocks ride and Lindsay's seven-year-old daughter, Hailey, was also starting in endurance rides. She and Natalie had instantly bonded, and Natalie had appreciated Lindsay's advice about the Tevis Cup, especially since Lindsay had seven Tevis buckles and had won the coveted Haggin Cup on Monk the previous year. Lindsay was going at a slower pace this year to give her friend a chance to experience the ride and earn her first Tevis buckle.

"Hey, Lindsay," Natalie called out to her friend. "Other than being steep, what's this section of trail like?"

Lindsay laughed as she replied, "I have absolutely no idea! I've always ridden it in daylight!"

Lindsay was usually among the elite group of riders who were far enough ahead that they had the benefit of riding the California Street Trail while there was still daylight. It was an entirely different Tevis experience for the riders at the front of the pack than the ones toward the back. As it turned out, this was the part of the trail where Brave would shine. As a gaited Saddlebred, he was able to cover the trail at a pace that made him a great leader for their small group. He moved out faster than a non-gaited horse could walk, but not so fast they had to trot the precarious parts of the trail too quickly. Brave naturally slowed down when the footing was bad and immediately picked up the pace as the footing improved.

Natalie and Kyla turned off the fairy lights once they got onto the trail and allowed the horses to use their natural night vision. Natalie handed over the decision-making to Brave, knowing he would take care of her. Riding in the pitch-black night on the switchbacks was similar to being on a roller coaster in a long, dark tunnel. Natalie had no idea which direction Brave was going next, and instead of bracing herself for each turn, she relaxed and found herself moving with him intuitively, their bodies and minds so closely connected it felt as if they were joined together, floating along in the darkness.

Giving up control was not something that came naturally to this passionate mother of four. She was used to being the rock for her family. The glue that held the craziness together, and in some messy, noisy, beautiful way, kept their lives on track and heading in the right direction. She and Adam taught their children that life was a string of experiences, some big, some small, but all to be celebrated and approached with the premise that the Lord would take care of them if they fed the fires of their faith. Natalie wanted to protect Kyla from her fears on this section of the trail, but she also wanted Kyla to experience handing her fears over to God and trust that He, and Flash, would not only see her through this, but would show her the immense glory that could be found when she released the reins and rode down the mountain in the space between heaven and earth.

Kyla followed her mother's lead and let go, and in that release she found a strength in herself that she had never known was there. She and Flash floated through the night, weaving down the series of switchbacks, zigzagging down the mountainside as the night accepted them as one of its own. It was mesmerizing and magical, and the girls both knew they were privileged to be a part of that moment. God's hand was at work here.

When Natalie eventually turned to look behind her, she realized they were now leading a whole line of horses and riders who had fallen in behind them and had been relying on Brave to lead them safely down the mountain. Natalie reached down and petted his warm, thick neck, thanking him for all he was giving her that night. She marveled again at her large Saddlebred horse and the tiny Hackney pony. What a special gift these two amazing creatures had been to their family.

The horses stopped to drink from the water troughs at the intersection of trail that marked the beginning of Cal 2, historically known as Peachstone. As soon as the horses had finished drinking, they continued toward Ford's Bar with Brave once again taking the lead, closely followed by Flash with Bucephalos and Monk right behind him. Lindsay was impressed with the energetic way Flash moved and with the confidence of his rider. Brave was also looking strong, and Lindsay laughed as she remembered a nervous Natalie asking her a month before Tevis whether she thought Brave and Flash could make it through this ride. It was pretty obvious they were both holding their own against the Tevis trail.

The steep switchbacks finally ended, and they were now trotting along a hard packed gravel road that would lead them into Francisco's vet check when, for no apparent reason, Bucephalos took a hard fall and landed on his knees, sliding along the trail as he ground to a halt. He was a handsome horse, but even at twenty-three years old he didn't have the Tevis experience of Monk, his famous offspring. In fact, it had been questionable whether Bucephalos would even make it to Tevis that year, as seven weeks prior he had been galloping around his paddock and taken a nasty spill. It looked as if he had severely damaged his neck, and for a terrible moment Lindsay thought she may have to have him euthanized. Fortunately, the injury was not as bad as it had first seemed and he had made a full recovery. But now he had fallen again, and his face and knees had taken the brunt of it.

Bucephalos managed to pull himself back to his feet, and Lindsay grabbed a flashlight from her saddle bags to check for injuries. The skin on his knees was scraped up with road rash. Lindsay only saw minor bleeding and didn't think it was anything serious, but she wouldn't know for sure until she felt how he moved out. They were so close to

Francisco's vet check that Lindsay rode him in at a walk, glad to see that he appeared sound. The whole group slowed to walk in with her. Flash wasn't happy to be asked to go at a pace slower than a trot, and Lindsay found it was a good distraction to watch Flash trotting ahead of them with Kyla turning him in circles to slow him down in order to stay with the group. She marveled at the energy the little horse had after eighty-five miles of tough going. He really was an anomaly.

It wasn't long before they saw the heart-warming sight of Francisco's vet check. Volunteers had lit up the area with white Christmas lights, which looked strange but welcoming in what felt like the middle of nowhere. Volunteers offered to hold the horses so the weary riders could take a break or go to the bathroom while others brought pans of mash for the horses and plates of food to tempt the humans.

Nancy, riding her first Tevis on Monk, had been suffering from terrible vertigo and motion sickness from the constant movement of riding in the dark. It produced a feeling that lingered even when a rider dismounted and sat on the ground. It was not uncommon to find riders mentally struggling with getting back out on the trail knowing how debilitated they would be. Lindsay and Nancy decided to take a little longer at this vet check and give both Nancy and Bucephalos a chance to regroup. In fact, when Lindsay got Bucephalos into the light she could see that the poor horse also had road rash from his nose to his forehead. After being cleaned up he was fine to continue, but for a moment Lindsay wondered if being pulled at Francisco's would have been all that bad. She was feeling the exhaustion from being out on the course so much longer than usual, as well as the added pressure of helping another rider get their first completion. The thought was fleeting. She knew that once they successfully crossed the finish line in fifteen miles everything they were going through would have been worth it.

Natalie and Kyla were feeling fine, although both were starting to feel tired. They had entered the vet check at 12:50 a.m. Incredibly, Brave pulsed down two minutes before Flash, but as usual, Flash's overall vet scores were slightly better. Flash had most likely been frustrated at having to slow down the last two miles, and that had caused his heart rate go up. He obviously wasn't tired. Natalie and Kyla were thrilled to see both horses get an A for both attitude and impulsion, and both horses ate ravenously and drank deeply.

Without the company of Lindsay and Nancy, Natalie realized it was up to her and Kyla to reach the finish line by themselves. Kyla was nervous to ride back out onto the dark trail alone with only her mother for company. The chatter and the sound of multiple hoofbeats when riding in a group made the shadows and night noises easier for her to tolerate. Now the silence was deafening. Natalie rode ahead and Kyla followed, trying to shake the feeling that she was being watched from the bushes, and that at any moment the creatures of the night could leap out and attack. She was terrified. As a girl with an extremely active imagination, it wasn't long before she began to hallucinate. There are many stories of endurance athletes hallucinating in the dark, especially toward the end of a long race. Kyla was mentally feeling the strain of the long day and the miles that seemed to go on forever. The shadows around her began to shift and take on unusual shapes. She saw a tree become the shape of a fox and imagined a forest full of foxes rushing out at her and Flash as they passed. When she looked ahead at her mother for comfort, her mother had become a scary monster with eyes staring back at her through the darkness. Part of her brain knew she was hallucinating, but in that moment, in the middle of the night, it all seemed very real. She felt alone and surrounded by dangers that threatened to harm her and Flash. She was too scared to even cry out for help and rode on through the darkness, having no option but to keep moving forward, hoping to make it out of the haunted forest unscathed.

Kyla was thankful when they caught up with another rider on the trail. Reality snapped her back to the present, and she realized she had merely fallen into that strange state of consciousness where reality and fantasy merge and play tricks on a tired mind. The person they encountered was Molly Pearson, a first-time Tevis rider but no stranger to competing in feats of endurance with horses. In 2019 Molly completed the grueling Mongolian Derby, which extends over 1,000 kilometers through the Mongolian steppe. Riders change horses every forty kilometers and take ten days to complete the race. The Mongolian Derby horses are semi-wild, sturdy, fearless, diminutive, and unbelievably tough. Sort of like Flash.

Molly was not enjoying her Tevis experience. She was on Radar, a borrowed horse, and it had been a last-minute option to ride him at Tevis that year when another rider pulled out of the race. She was using the owner's tack, and the stirrups had been very slightly twisting her ankles for the past eighty-five miles. Her ankles were now screaming at her every single second of the ride. Molly had taken a couple of Advil at Foresthill but nothing since, and the constant pain was making her nauseous. Although the Mongolian Derby had many long, miserable stretches, they had been broken up with stopovers to eat yak butter with the locals and to change horses every forty kilometers. In between the ten to twelve hours of riding a day, she had been able to do that most wonderful thing of all—sleep. Tevis, on the other hand, took place over a concentrated period of time, and for her it was a concentrated period of utter misery. By the time Molly had reached Foresthill, she was already asking herself why she was doing this. She told her crew that if she ever, for even a moment, considered doing Tevis again they were to remind her of how horrible she felt in that moment. However, there was no question of quitting. Molly wasn't going to let thirty-four miles stand between her and a Tevis buckle. In her mind she had barely more than an LD—a limited distance endurance ride—up ahead. Molly's horse was a seasoned competitor with several Tevis ride completions, including a top ten, and Molly knew he had a strong chance of finishing. She would do everything she could to finish, even though she knew that the miles between now and then would be the most painful of her competitive riding career.

The least painful pace for Molly was keeping Radar at a walk, and she had left Francisco's at a slow and easy pace. By the time Natalie and Kyla caught up to her, Molly knew that she wouldn't finish in time if she didn't speed up. She allowed Natalie and Kyla to pass and then tucked in behind them. Natalie knew that some people might have had a problem with her "drafting" off them, especially so close to the end of the ride, but Natalie didn't say anything to discourage her, and Molly distracted herself as much as possible by watching Flash perkily trotting down the trail ahead of her. She loved listening to Natalie and Kyla's banter as they rode along, and the three of them paced well together. She had not officially introduced herself to the mother and daughter team yet, but that would change as they navigated the next river crossing.

They needed to keep moving, always aware that the clock was ticking down closer to the time they needed to cross the finish line to get a completion. It was just nine miles to the next checkpoint of Lower Quarry, then six miles to the finish. They headed west along the north side of the river. Once they hit a primitive wagon road the trees thinned out enough to allow the moonlight to break through. Brave fell into an easy canter, the river moving and gleaming alongside them; the easy ground offering some relief to their horses' legs after the miles of challenging hills. Brave naturally chose the pace that he felt was most suitable, and Natalie let him stretch out his muscles and enjoy the second wind that he seemed to be feeling.

When riding, almost every muscle in the rider's body is engaged to ride in a balanced manner. Every step is a dance between horse and rider, each feeding off the other's movements and energy. A horse and rider team who have worked together over an extended period work together almost telepathically—reading each other's thoughts and responding to every situation with total synergy.

Flash, cantering alongside them, never faltered for even a minute. His one moment of looking tired halfway through the ride had come and gone. The pony was a machine, eating up the miles with no sign of slowing down, confidently carrying his rider through the night. And Molly stayed with them, Radar having no problem keeping up while Molly gritted her teeth and tried not to pass out from the pain. The moment was less magical for her.

Before long, the three horses approached the sandy riverbank of the river crossing where green glow lights laid out a path through the river for them to follow. Even here volunteers waited for the competitors. They offered Molly a shot of Fireball Cinnamon Whisky to ease the pain from her ankle, which she politely declined, so they held a Gatorade out to her instead. Molly felt nauseous and nothing appealed to her, but she must have looked awful because Natalie shouted across to her, "Take the Gatorade, lady. You need it!"

It was the first time Natalie had really looked at Molly, and she could tell that she was in trouble. Natalie hoped that she could last the few miles to the finish. At this point, there seemed to be a 50/50 chance.

Just ahead was the final river crossing. Even though Brave was used to seeing the green glow sticks along the course, he was not sure about the ones below the river's surface, and he refused to go in. Molly's horse didn't want to go in either, even though he had encountered them in prior years, and even Flash thought the river crossing was a bad idea. Eventually, Natalie got Brave to step into the water, and the others tentatively followed. As the river became deeper, Kyla tried to keep her legs and feet out of the chilly water. She tucked her heels under her bottom and lifted the fleece covered stirrup leathers across the front of the saddle. She could have joined a trick rider team with her efforts to stay dry. As Flash surged through the water that threatened to soak his saddle blanket, Kyla's legs slipped and made contact. She knew that riding the rest of the way with wet shoes and socks wouldn't feel good, but that was one of the risks of riding a very short horse. It was a relief when all three horses emerged from the river, shook off the excess water, and picked up the trail to the Lower Quarry vet check.

CHAPTER 18

A Perfect Ending to
a New Beginning

*"Everything is within your power,
and your power is within you."*

—JANICE TRACHTMAN

They reached Lower Quarry and were surprised to see so many horse and rider teams there, seemingly in no rush to continue. Like Nancy, many riders were suffering from motion sickness, while others were just plain exhausted. The hard-working volunteers were doing everything they could to comfort and encourage the riders, simultaneously making sure their horses were fed and watered. They knew from experience that some of the riders laying on the ground looking like they would never recover would be riding across the finish line thirty minutes from now with their arms raised in victory! Endurance riders are a strange but tough breed of human.

Natalie glanced over and was surprised to see John once again. It seemed like another lifetime ago that he had glued on Flash's boots. The distance, the hours in the saddle, being awake in the middle of the night—all these things contributed to a sense of being in another time and place, an alternative universe. Natalie and John congratulated each other for getting this far, hesitant to celebrate too early but feeling the swell of anticipation of crossing the finish line a few miles ahead.

It was now 3:16 a.m. as they left the lights of Lower Quarry and headed into the darkness one last time. They looked around for Molly but couldn't see her and figured she had chosen to stay there longer because of her ankles.

Molly had asked a volunteer to trot her horse out for the vet, as she simply couldn't run with the pain she was in. She must have still looked terrible because several volunteers were approaching her and trying to persuade her to eat and drink, but she declined everything except a single M&M. She knew she needed to eat, but she was worried she would start vomiting. A kind volunteer helped her mount her horse, wondering how on earth she would be able to finish the ride in her current state. It was fortunate that the vets were only concerned with the horses and weren't checking that their riders were fit to continue—Molly would have been pulled, for sure.

As she left the vet check, she desperately wanted to catch up to her new friends again. She couldn't imagine suffering through the next six miles alone. Natalie and Kyla were glad to see her pull in behind them.

"How are you doing?" Kyla asked Molly.

"Oh, just wonderful. Almost there, right?" Molly replied as she gritted her teeth through the pain and hoped she didn't pass out before the finish.

The three of them traveled along a road that paralleled the river and led to Highway 49, a strange sign of civilization that announced the beginning of their return to real life after hours of living in the Tevis bubble. Volunteers were stopping any passing traffic so the horses could cross the highway safely. Up ahead the riders would cross the famous Western States Trail landmark of No Hands Bridge with the American River flowing a good distance below. As they approached the bridge, they saw that a few people had hiked down from the highway to cheer on the horses as they emerged from the trail. The horses didn't hesitate as they trotted their way confidently across the bridge, rejoining the trail on the other side.

Crossing the bridge seemed to make the upcoming finish line seem very real. Kyla knew at this point that Flash had thankfully experienced no issues carrying her, and she felt herself relax for the first time in a long while. The journey through the darkness was almost over, and she hadn't even realized how much tension she had been holding inside. Here they were, at four in the morning, with just four miles to go!

The trail began climbing again, a more gradual climb beside the river. The trail then split off, narrowing once more before reaching Robie Point. As Natalie, Kyla, and Molly crested Robie Point, they felt a sense of disappointment. They had forgotten they still had to pass through this area—a cul-de-sac at the end of a residential road that dissected the trail for thirty feet or so. They had been hoping the approach to Robie Point had been the final climb to the finish line. The horses tanked up from the water troughs that had been placed there and picked up the trail one last time. The finish was so close they could taste it.

Molly had been happy for their slower pace as they covered this section of trail. Her ankle remained inflamed, and she felt the overwhelming need to be done. She had been pressing her thighs against the saddle to assist with posting at a trot as much as possible, but at ninety-eight miles her muscles were so tired that she could only sit on her horse like a sack of potatoes, sending him a silent apology for how she was riding.

It was amazing to think how far they had come since that morning—well, the previous morning, really. They had traversed ninety-eight miles across the Sierra Nevada Mountain range, conquering 14,800 feet of elevation gain and 22,900 feet of elevation loss. They had forgotten the faces of the volunteers who had helped them along the way, but they would never forget their kindness. It takes more than a village to put on a ride like the Tevis. It takes a whole town—many of them, in fact. Chuck Stalley, the race director, had seemed to be in one hundred different places that day. He popped up everywhere, checking every detail, meeting with everyone who ran the vet checks and extending his thanks. He was called on for every emergency, big and small, and he, like so many others, was running an endurance event of his own behind the scenes.

Since 1955, horses had crossed this trail, and they had given their all to the riders who asked it of them. Brave and Flash were no different. With every stride they took, they carried their riders closer and closer to the finish line, knowing they were close to the comfortable stalls of the fairgrounds just up ahead.

The trail offered a few more places to trip and fall as the horses climbed toward the finish, but they didn't take one misstep. To Natalie and Kyla, it felt as if they were soaring along the trail, gliding upward toward the lights they could faintly see through the trees. There were people in front of the three of them now. They were moving slower than Brave and Flash wished to go, but no one was about to move off the trail and give up their placing so close to the finish.

"Isn't this where Flash was almost bitten by the rattlesnake?" Kyla asked.

Natalie laughed. "Yes, but don't worry. You're not in front this time!"

As Kyla followed behind her mother, she thought about the little pony she first met all those years ago. The one that shook with fear. The one that feared the sound of a human's voice and who had stood trembling in the back of his pen. She thought of the five hundred dollars she had saved to buy this pony and how it had been a race against time whether she would be able to bring him to Tevis, as her young bones had stretched and grown, making her taller; too tall, perhaps, for what she had asked him to do.

But it had been faith that got them to this point. Shelah Wetter's faith that Flash had the heart and the ability to still carry his rider, Natalie's faith that the Lord would guide them both and keep them safe on this journey together, and Kyla's faith, in herself, in God, and in her love for this little pony, that had given her the strength to overcome her fears and conquer this trail.

Kyla reached down and put her arms around her pony's neck as she whispered, "I knew you could do it, Flash. I knew it!"

How strange that when Flash had been scared, Kyla had been there to teach him about the strength of love and how to overcome his fears, and now, in the past twenty-three hours, he had done the same for her. Kyla didn't think that Flash had ever doubted they would finish. He didn't even seem tired. He was just taking his girl home.

They heard the murmuring of voices becoming louder as they got closer. "Is someone coming?" the voices asked. "Is it the pony? My gosh, it is! Look at him!"

Team Law emerged into the clearing. Lights shone upon the banner that hung over the finish line. They glanced at the clock, which flashed their official finish time in neon red: 4:33 a.m. They called their numbers one last time to the finish line officials and watched the horses take a long drink from the round stone trough where even the goldfish didn't faze the horses anymore. They had finished with forty-two minutes to spare.

The crew was there waiting for them. Adam, so proud of his girls. James and Wynona, who were amazed at what their daughter and granddaughter had accomplished. And Kacey and Shelah, who had kept them all safe and sane throughout the long day and night. Kacey had tears in her eyes. She couldn't believe she had ever doubted this little pony who had shown so much bravery and heart that day.

As they rode down to the stadium, Natalie and Kyla looked over at each other and smiled. They had made it. Both horses were sound on the tarmac road and were bright eyed as they saw the lights from the stadium and heard the murmuring of the crowd in the distance. Natalie reached out to her daughter and Kyla reached across the space between them, taking her mother's hand. Natalie wanted to freeze that moment forever. She knew that would be one of the most perfect moments of her whole life. For a mother, that moment meant everything.

They made a sharp left. Seeing the brightly lit stadium ahead, the realization finally sank in: they were almost done. They had completed the miles, but they still had to do their victory lap and vet through one last time.

Natalie didn't want Brave to get his heart rate up before the final vet check and was hesitant to let him do his victory lap at more than a slow gait around the track. But Kyla wanted to canter her victory lap with Flash in celebration. Natalie worried that if Kyla was behind her, the ride photographer wouldn't get a clear shot of Flash passing under the banner. All this seemed very logical to Natalie at the time, but afterwards she wondered why she didn't just let Kyla and Flash fly around the track together. After all, it would be the very last time they could celebrate a victory like this together and they deserved it. They argued right up until they were entering the stadium, and then somehow it all sorted itself out and they crossed under the Tevis banner to claim thirty-sixth and thirty-seventh place.

Both horses vetted through well and got their completion. There were no more hurdles to cross, no more doubts to have, and no more time clocks to outrun. They would be receiving their Tevis buckles only a few hours from now at the Tevis Cup Award Banquet and Ceremony. Out of 133 horse and rider teams only 63 teams finished. Was it beginners' luck? Their extraordinary horses? The miles of XP rides they had completed? Or had it been their prayers along the way and the faith that Natalie and Kyla had both held onto throughout their journey? Maybe it was a perfect combination of all these factors.

Once Natalie and Kyla knew that they had officially finished, the tiredness became overwhelming. Shelah and Kacey offered to take the horses and settle them into their stalls. Natalie was glad that she had chosen these people she trusted so well for their crew. It was hard to leave the horses who had been their constant companions all day and night, and who had given them so much simply because they had asked. But knowing they were in such excellent hands made the separation easier. The crew's job would continue until the horses had been fed, watered, brushed, and blanketed, and had their legs wrapped to prevent swelling from the long miles. The horses would also need to be presented to the vets for their one-hour post-ride check back at the stadium. For hours after the last finishers had come in, the dedicated vets would walk the barns, checking on the horses resting there, making sure that each was comfortable and recovering from their one-hundred-mile journey.

The official cut-off time for finishing was 5:15 a.m. on July 25, and a few souls would feel the bleak disappointment of going the distance and not receiving a completion at the end for being overtime. Others would finish in time, only to have their hopes dashed when their horses failed the final vet check. The Western States Trail was not kind to everyone who traveled upon her, but she always left an indelible memory that drew people back to her regardless.

There is no such thing as failure when it comes to the Tevis Cup ride, even for those who don't win their buckles that day. Competing in the Tevis Cup truly is about the journey. The physical journey across the mountains and the inner journey the soul experiences along the way. Rarely does a rider express regret at having stepped up to the starting line at this most iconic of rides; most are simply thankful for the chance to try.

Kyla and Natalie desperately needed some sleep before the awards ceremony that would take place in just a few short hours, and they hurried back to the Airbnb to shower and fall into bed. The reality that they had earned their Tevis buckle had still not sunk in. All they could focus on were the hot showers and warm beds awaiting them, not the trail they had just left behind.

After the best shower in the world, Kyla climbed into bed and whispered a prayer of thanks. Despite how tired she was, she knew that it was only fitting that she show gratitude for all the gifts she had been given that day. A strange feeling of peace came over her, and she felt a lightness take over her being. She had thought she would be sad, knowing that her final adventure with Flash was over, but instead she felt the warm glow of the Holy Spirit bathe her, a feeling she had been searching for but had only felt in the shadow of her parents. Now, her own spirit was lifted and healed, the connection to God so complete and so beautiful that she suddenly realized the answer to her search of who she was. It had been there all the time; she just had to find it. The temple is often compared to the mountains, and in the mountains that day, Kyla had found her answer.

She was a child of God, and she always would be.

• • •

As Natalie climbed into the shower, the dirt from the Tevis trail draining away, she felt as if her body was still in motion; appropriate really, since she had been on "Mo Motion Jack" for almost twenty-four hours. The bed seemed like the best place in the world to be, but before she could climb into it, she needed to check once more on her daughter, who she hadn't been apart from for more than a few minutes in the last twenty-four hours. Natalie thought of every smile, every look of fear, every moment of amazement that had passed across her daughter's face and knew without a doubt that she would always hold this day in her heart. Tevis wasn't just another race or even just an experience. It was a moment in time that had allowed her and her daughter to synchronize their souls as they journeyed across a part of history.

The trail was kept alive by those who gave their all to conquer it, although maybe conquer wasn't the right word, since all those who traveled the Western States Trail became an indelible part of her story; a story that had spanned centuries and that would continue to span more with the help of all those who treasured and protected her.

Kyla was sleeping soundly, hugging the covers under her chin and breathing lightly, her sweet face looking rested and peaceful. Natalie gently swept a stray lock of hair back from across her face where it had fallen, and smiled. For the past twenty-four hours, Natalie and Kyla had existed in a wonderful place, set apart from everything else that was going on in the world. They had relied on each other, God, and their magnificent horses to carry them forward. Always forward. Never hurry, never tarry. Natalie had experienced more with her daughter in one day than most mothers were blessed with in a lifetime, and she would always be grateful for that. She knew there were years ahead where they may not be as connected as they had been that day—raising teenagers was its own kind of endurance event—but those Tevis memories would bind them together always.

Natalie climbed into her own bed and finally—*finally*—closed her eyes. Before falling asleep she said one last prayer of thanks. God had been with them on their journey. In fact, He had been with them ever since the moment that Kyla had first laid eyes on that pony.

There had been a plan, all along.

EPILOGUE

CLAIRE ECKARD, DECEMBER 17, 2021

The Tevis trail is one hundred miles of magic and history, born from the necessity of crossing the mountains, and preserved to honor those who have become a part of her. For the crews and the bystanders, you sit in the dark at the finish line, waiting for the teams to crawl out of a tunnel of darkness, realizing they have struggled, bled, cried, and persevered to reach that final moment, and knowing that every person—whether this is their first or thirty-first completion—has been changed, reborn in some way from their experience that day. The trail has been trampled and torn, worshiped and hated, loved and ultimately accepted for who she is; the beautiful vessel that inspires dreams, gives them life, and touches your soul before finally releasing you from her spell. You emerge from her depths with a different perspective of what *life* is, who *you* are, and for a moment you are glad to finally be free of her, to recover from the suffering, but all the while knowing you will be called back: a prodigal child returning home to Mother Earth.

I was at Tevis that year. I have never ridden it myself, but I have crewed multiple times for my husband and friends when they have competed it. I have developed a deep passion for the Tevis Cup and its history. There's an indescribable aura that surrounds the Tevis trail, and you don't necessarily have to do the ride to be swept up by her, knowing you are in the presence of greatness.

This year, for once, I wasn't crewing and was able to move around freely, without committing to a job. I was in the middle of writing a trilogy, *The Gallant Series*, with the first one—*Gallant, The Call of The Trail*—being published that fall. The last book in the trilogy brings the fictional characters to Tevis, so I had a vested interest in paying extra attention to everything that year and absorbing all that was going on in ride camp and at the vet checks—little details that I may have missed in previous years.

The year Kyla and Flash did Tevis, I was sitting with ninety-seven-year-old Julie Suhr, the Grande Dame of endurance, at the top of Bath Road in Foresthill—a place she had passed through many times while earning her twenty-two silver Tevis buckles. I am sure memories of the many horses who had carried her across those mountains filled her mind as she watched eagerly to see how each horse was doing as it made its way up Bath Road to the sixty-eight-mile vet check at Foresthill.

Having studied the history of the trail, stories filled my mind—of how these horses were following in the footsteps of all those who had done this ride before them, adding their names to a venerable list of athletes since 1955, as well as the ghosts of those who had travelled across the Emigrant Trail, risking everything in their search for gold in these mountains. For these modern-day pioneers the trail has unearthed a joy, a determination, an immense gratitude, and a self-awareness of what the human spirit can achieve when it is faced with suffering, sweat, tears, and promises of what they'll earn once the journey is over. For some, dreams will die out there, only to be resurrected once again as the ride entries for the following year became available. For others, stepping across the finish line will be a highlight of their life achievements, the silver belt buckle worn proudly from that day forth to signify the day the High Sierras accepted them as one of her own.

There was a strange feeling of nostalgia, mingled with overwhelming respect for those who had made it to the start of the race the early morning of July 24, 2021. I knew many of the riders personally, having been involved in the sport of endurance myself for over twenty years. I had never met Natalie and Kyla, other than following their adventures with Flash on his Facebook page.

Julie was getting tired, so we packed up our chairs and headed back to the hotel in Auburn. I didn't see the mother and daughter team of Natalie and Kyla Law as they came off the trail and entered the vet check at Foresthill, but I knew they were there, somewhere, making their way along the course, and I hoped they weren't among the many that would be pulled that day. By the next morning I knew they had finished, and Julie and I were so happy for the young girl and her pony as we watched Kyla and Natalie cross the stage to accept their silver belt buckles.

Shelah Wetter once said that there was nothing special about Kyla and Flash, other than the fact that they stuck it out through *everything*, and *that* is what made them special. Now that I know them both, I can see that they were obviously put into each other's life for a reason. There's a magic between them; a bond that binds them like an invisible thread. So long as one of them is still breathing I don't think that bond will be broken, even as Flash moves forward with a new partner in Layla. There's just something about the two of them together; Kyla and Flash.

Their race against time is over. Kyla has had another growth spurt and has grown another six inches since Tevis, while Flash is just as short as ever. In her own words, Kyla is "sad and heartbroken" about outgrowing him. She still finds it hard to see him and Layla together, but I know that as Kyla continues her own life journey, the lessons she learned from her adventures with Flash will always remain with her, helping her navigate through whatever trials, and trails, she will experience.

I am exceptionally proud to now call Natalie a friend. The woman is a fiercely determined and magnificent kind of being, although I do advise increasing your life insurance policy if you plan to hang out with her. She and Adam, without a doubt, will find many more adventures for their brood. When I last checked, the kids were offering adventure tours called "Hiking with Goats." Gabe has become a stellar chef specializing in English toffee, Emma is fishing her heart out, and Kyla's training horses for others and still enjoying spending time with Flash, her one-hundred-mile pony. I also recently found out that Adam is an exceptionally fine singer! Natalie is right there, orchestrating everything while still following her own passion for her horses. The family has no end of talents, and I believe that by allowing their children to explore their boundaries, Natalie and Adam are raising them to take life by the horns and live it to the fullest. I have an immense amount of affection for this wild and wonderful group of people.

As for Layla, well, she's only nine years old, and who knows what Flash has planned for her future. He's still the one making most of the decisions, but she's beginning to win some of the battles. I have no doubt that if she gives as much time to their partnership as Kyla did, Flash will eventually come around to accepting her as the special girl that she is. If you want to follow their adventures, don't forget to join Flash's Facebook page, The Adventures of Flash, the Hackney Pony. In the meantime, just remember to move out of the way if you see her screaming down a trail near you!

Kyla and I still have lots of work to do together in order to share their story once it is published. I am glad that we will be able to enjoy each other's company at the events and signings that we will be attending. We are even going to try and have Flash with us at some of them! You can find a list of our events on my website: ClaireEckardAuthor.com. I am so looking forward to the rest of my own journey with Kyla, Flash, and the rest of the Law family. Every moment with them is an amazing adventure!

Kyla has been an integral part of putting this book together, and I am amazed at her honesty and sharp mind. She's creative, thoughtful, tenacious, and is growing from a wonderful young girl into a truly lovely young lady with a very special heart. Kyla and Flash's journey, and of course that of Natalie and Brave, have become an integral part of the Tevis trail now, just like all those who have journeyed across it. I think they have given a little piece of themselves to the trail; a sort of sacrifice to that magnificent one-hundred-mile stretch of dirt reaching across the Sierras and tempting endurance athletes everywhere to do the same. The trail is fiercely protected by all those who touch her, and while Mother Nature often pops up to remind us all exactly who is in charge, that's just part of the untamed beauty drawing us all into her story. I hope the Laws have not seen the last of her. I suspect they will be back, as are most of those whose lives experience the trail.

Numerous people have sent Kyla and Flash congratulatory messages, including endurance royalty and the Utah senator, Mike Lee. They have been featured in magazines, documentaries, and podcasts. Kyla has only just begun to realize what they accomplished together, and it is helping to soften the harsh reality that her days of riding Flash are over. Looking back, those one hundred miles across the Western States Trail with her mother by her side, her precious pony beneath her, gave Kyla so much more than knowing she simply finished an endurance ride. She has captured a thousand memories with her mother from their hours in the saddle, and now she can sit back and savor them all. She has overcome fear and adversity, taking on the darkness and pushing forward with the understanding that her faith will never let her down. Knowing that she is a child of God will serve her well in her future life adventures and guide her heart to make sure that she doesn't hurt others the way they hurt her.

Natalie and Adam are proud parents. They have seen their daughter take on the challenge of taming a wild pony, and then watched the pair succeed at the toughest endurance race in the world. Natalie is also proud of her amazing Brave. He lived up to his name and carried her along on the journey with her daughter, and she will always be forever grateful to him for that precious gift.

According to Chuck Stalley, Flash is indeed the smallest pony on record to ever officially complete the one-hundred mile Western States Trail Ride. His hoof beats have been heard from Lake Tahoe to Auburn. He has partied with the big boys! His name and Kyla's will be inscribed on the Scripps Foundation Cup as one of the few junior riders to complete the Tevis Cup.

This adventure may be over, but with Flash around, there are always new adventures just waiting to happen. The saying that great things often come in small packages has never been so true as with Flash, the Hackney pony!

ABOUT THE AUTHOR

Claire Eckard is an award-winning author whose books often highlight the extraordinary relationship between humans and animals. She grew up in England and travels there regularly, where she is still obsessed with clotted cream teas and the tranquil English countryside of her youth.

Claire and her husband own a ranch in Arizona with ten horses and a miniature mule with a bad attitude. She has two grown sons and two beautiful granddaughters. Claire has competed in endurance riding for many years and is a member of the American Endurance Ride Conference.

Kyla Law and Claire Eckard in Utah (2021)

Scan to visit

ClaireEckardAuthor.com

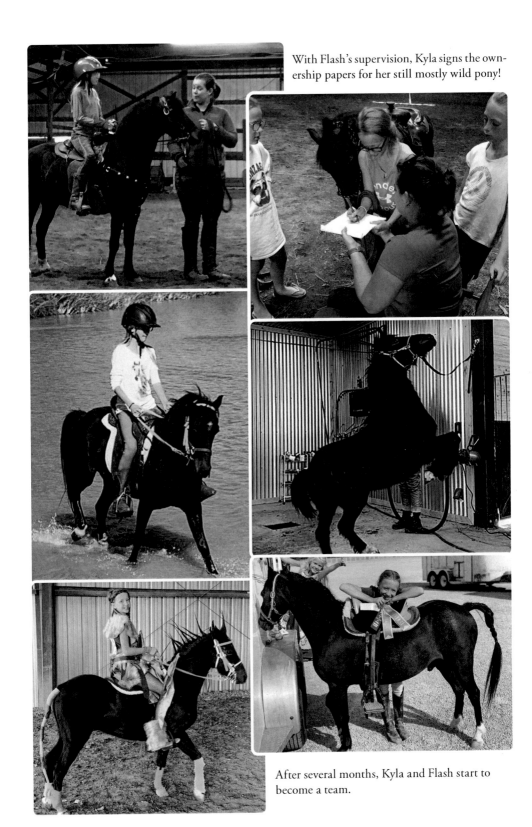

With Flash's supervision, Kyla signs the ownership papers for her still mostly wild pony!

After several months, Kyla and Flash start to become a team.

Photo credit: © Gore/Baylor Photography—Bill Gore

Photo credit: © Gore/Baylor Photography—Amy Olmstead

Photo credit: © Gore/Baylor Photography—Amy Olmstead

Top left: An unhappy Flash getting his special boots glued on. Top right: Kyla and Flash trot out for the vets at Robie Park. Bottom left: Leaving the Robinson Flat Vet Check. Bottom right: Taking on the famous Cougar Rock.

Top left: Best friends share a mash at the vet check. Top right: The start of the infamous Canyons. Bottom left: Still smiling near Elephant's Trunk. Bottom right: An eight-minute power nap at Foresthill.

"Natalie was determined to remain as positive and supportive as she could for her daughter in the miles ahead. She wrapped her arms around her daughter and held her close, comforting her and letting her know that she would never be alone. Not on this ride, not in the days afterward, and not for the rest of her life."

The Western States Trail Ride

FINISH

The Tevis Cup 100 miles - One Day Ride

Photo credit: © Gore/Baylor Photography—Bill Gore

The Western States Trail Ride

FINISH

The Tevis Cup 100 miles - One Day Ride

Photo credit: © Gore/Baylor Photography—Bill Gore

Top left: One hundred miles of trail completed and an official Tevis Cup finish. Natalie and Kyla stand elated and exhausted at the stadium in Auburn with crew members Kacey Oar and Shelah Wetter.

Middle: The official ride map of the Tevis Cup 100-mile One-Day Trail Ride, showing the check points and elevation gain and loss.

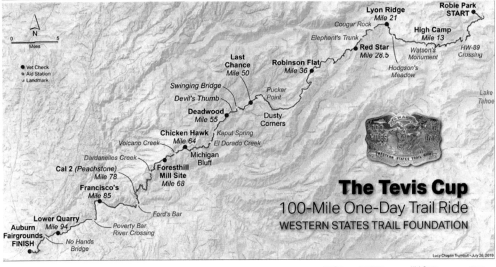

Bottom right: Kyla and Layla Law proudly wearing their first- and second-place junior award jackets respectively from the American Endurance Ride Conference (AERC).